Sixteen
SCANDALS

Sixteen
SCANDALS

20 Years of Sex, Lies and Other Habits of Our Great Leaders

A Musical Comedy of Errors from the CAPITOL STEPS

William Strauss and Elaina Newport

sourcebooks mediaFusion

An Imprint of Sourcebooks Inc.®
Naperville, Illinois

Published by Sourcebooks, Inc.
P.O. Box 4410, Naperville, Illinois 60567-4410
(630) 961-3900
FAX: (630) 961-2168
www.sourcebooks.com

Library of Congress Cataloging-in-Publication Data

Strauss, William.
Sixteen scandals : twenty years of sex, lies, and other habits of our
great leaders / William Strauss and Elaina Newport; a musical comedy of
errors from the Capitol Steps.
     p. cm.
ISBN 1-4022-0315-2 (paperback)
1. United States—Politics and government—1989—Humor. 2. United
States—Politics and government—1981–1989—Humor. 3. Scandals—United
States—History—20th century—Humor. 4. Political satire, American.
I. Title: 16 scandals. II. Newport, Elaina. III. Capitol Steps (Comedy
troupe) IV. Title.
E839.5 .S818 2002
973.92—dc21

                                                          2002006922

               Printed and bound in the United States of America
                 LB   10   9   8   7   6   5   4   3   2   1

To America's politicians—for being good sports

Contents

CD Track List

1

Fools on the Hill
("Superfranticunproductivenothinglegislation")

★★★★★★★★★
TRACKS: 1–3

America has a great sense of humor. It's one of the reasons we're a great country.

Our Bill of Rights gives us the freedom to laugh, and to make others laugh—but beyond that, there's a broad-shouldered quality to our nation, our leaders, and our people, a capacity not just to tell a joke, but to *take* one too.

Twenty years ago, we joined with some other U.S. Senate staffers to form a political satire troupe, the Capitol Steps. At first, this was just an office party. It soon became a hobby, then a small business, eventually a national touring company. We started when Ronald Reagan had just been elected president, and since then we've

TRACK: 2

★★★★★★★★★★★★★★

**Superfranticunproductive-
nothinglegislation
(parody of
"Supercalifragilisticexpialidocious")**

We senators and congressman are pulling
off a fast one

This legislative session is much slower than
the last one

Our list of great accomplishments is surely
not a vast one

Don't ask about our latest law, we really
haven't passed one

Superfranticunproductivenothinglegislation

Kosher pickle packing month deserves a
great oration

Never let important work disturb our next
vacation

Superfranticunproductivenothinglegislation

performed our show through four administrations (five if you count Hillary's), appeared onstage in forty-seven states (and New Jersey), and had a rollicking good time.

Along the way, we've learned a lot about humor and politics in a free society—and a thing or two about scandals.

Our leaders are imperfect people—aren't we all?—and our political institutions aren't perfect either. But, on the whole, our country is a pretty good place, which makes it all the more amusing when our presidents and Congresses screw things up. Their misdeeds become "scandals" not when they do them, but when they get *caught*.

Before a country's leaders can get snared by scandalous behavior, somebody's got to hold them accountable. In America, we do this, in part, by laughing at them. When we do, in a democracy, we're in effect laughing at ourselves. We expect our leaders to laugh at their own foibles too—and, mostly, they do. Americans have been that way since our country was founded.

Political satire is a powerful tradition here. That too dates back to the days of the Revolution, if not before.

Francis Hopkinson is one of our nation's lesser-known founders, but he set the early tone for our capacity to tell and take a political joke—to make fun out of foolishness.

He was a true Renaissance man—a classical composer, codesigner of the first American flag, signer of the Declaration of Independence, *and* political satirist. At the height of the Revolutionary War, Hopkinson tried to be a military genius, as well. He organized a totally crazy scheme to blow up British warships parked in Philadelphia harbor. He led a band of patriots up the Delaware River with wooden kegs filled with dynamite. They dropped the kegs in the water, with the hope that they would float into the British ships, explode, and sink the ships.

The plan was a total fiasco. The kegs succeeded only in providing some amusing target practice for the enemy. Afterwards, Hopkinson trumpeted his own little scandal throughout the colonies by writing a ditty, "The Battle of the Kegs," set to the well-known tune of "Maggie Lauder," one of those half-octave melodies with a bouncey rhythm that passed for pop music in those days. ("The cannons roar from shore to shore / The small arms make a rattle / Since wars began, I'm sure no man / E'er saw so strange a battle / The fish below swam to and fro / Attack'd from ev'ry quarter / Why sure, thought they, the devil's to pay / Among folks above the water.")

Was it funny? To patriots in the 1770s, probably so.

Had Hopkinson lived in our own time, he might have taken his act a few steps further, writing silly songs about George Washington's wooden teeth, John Adams's wooden personality, and Thomas Jefferson's very un-wooden sex life. But, instead, he went back to Pennsylvania and became a judge.

Fast forward two hundred years to our own time—and the scandal that gave us our name.

John Jenrette was a little-known South Carolina Congressman, married to a sexually athletic blonde bombshell Playmate-wannabe named Rita. In 1981, the two of them shared a kinky little marital moment behind the columns on the U.S. Capitol's east front, after which Rita chatted gaily to the media about how she and John had trysted "on the Capitol steps," and then added a few shocking details. "I had on a full-length coat that enveloped him," she explained on a morning talk show. "It was like being married to a rock star." She would soon reveal in *Playboy* exactly what lay hidden under that coat. But, unlike Hopkinson, neither John or Rita exposed their scandal in song.

That delicious task would fall to us.

Bill Strauss was thirty-four, a committee counsel and staff director, recently published author of two serious books, a sober-minded guy, more a smiler than laugher, who until then had sung only in the shower. Elaina Newport was twenty-five, an administrative assistant new to Capitol Hill who typed a mean keyboard, could write a monumental memo in minutes, and directed her hearty laugh at other people's jokes, not her own.

We were both on the staff of the United States Senate Subcommittee on Energy, Nuclear Proliferation, and Government Processes for the

United States Senate Committee of Governmental Affairs—a name that took three lines of ten-point type on our business cards.

And we were both news junkies. Serious news, top secret news (Bill had a "codeword" security clearance), and, of course, gossip. Much of what passed for "news" in our senatorial workplace pertained to scandalous sexcapades involving members of Congress. In the late '70s, two old power guys—Wilbur Mills and Wayne Hays—had quirky flings, Mills with stripper Fanne Foxe and Hays with a secretary who typed fifty words a month, Elizabeth Ray.

Those were the days when Ted Kennedy was in full prowl; rumors swirled about an "Attic Girl," who, so they say, regularly held court atop the Dirksen Senate Office Building with members, staffers, cops, and anybody else who dropped by; and tongues tut-tutted about the naughty conduct of teenage pages in a dorm once known as the Young Women's Christian Home that had come to be called (truth in labeling?) "Virgin Village."

Pardon us if we weren't surprised. Check the dictionary's last definition for what is meant by "congress." (*Hint*: It has more to do with the lower body than the upper body.)

While sex rumors were what passed for comic relief in the dense underbrush of the Washington jungle, a different kind of fun floated around the treetops, thanks to the ascension of a president and first lady who had actually been an actor and actress.

Ron and Nancy Reagan. We couldn't picture them having sex on the Capitol steps, or the White House steps, or maybe even at all. They weren't horny, just corny, always so busy buying designer White House wallpaper, clear-cutting redwoods, and slashing taxes for the rich and spending for the poor. Real side-splitting stuff.

After the stunning election of 1980, all of Washington felt a little slapstick. The Democrats had run both Houses of Congress for over a quarter century, but now Reagan's coattails had led his Grand Old Party back from the wilderness into control of the Senate. Republicans (including us) could now afford to be whimsical, an attitude long considered the sole province of Democrats. That's what power can do to you.

The year 1981 became the era of the official smiley sticker, with a new "aw shucks" tone set by the commander-in-chief. Many Americans were skeptical, wondering if Reagan's cheerfulness might just be a celluloid act, a *Bedtime for Bonzo* on the Potomac. We sang "Ronald R. Superstar / Who are you, how did you get so far?"

We were just coming off the ultra-earnest years of Jimmy Carter–style "malaise" and, besides, that peanut farmer of a president only felt lust in his heart. Ted Kennedy felt lust in his pants—now *that's* entertainment—but to the anguish of comedians, Jimmy had fended off Teddy to earn the chance to run for re-election and give America four more years of gloomy moralisms. Instead, he got crushed by a G.O.P. actor who had made a career out of being underestimated by others—including comedians.

At heart, Ronald Reagan revealed himself as more old-style entertainer than old-school statesman. "Hark when Gerald Ford was king / We were bored with everything," we would sing. "Now, with Ronald Reagan king / No one is bored with anything." Maybe that's why he won. That's also why, as a White House occupant, the new president was, as we sang in one of our early songs, a "perfect present resident" for anyone wanting to start a comedic troupe.

Curiously, the first lady's public persona was as cool as the president's was warm. "Where's the rest of me?" Reagan had asked in a film in which his legs had been chopped off. Well, that's what Nancy knew how to do: chop off the legs of anyone who said anything unkind about her husband, even in jest. You could see shades of this in her own film roles, when she was Nancy Davis. An actress adept at flashing her eyes from sad to hard without ever passing through friendly.

Through 1981, Reagan's first year as president, such was the sense of humor in the city in which we labored. The chairman of our subcommittee was Senator Charles H. Percy of Illinois, who also chaired the United States Senate Committee on Foreign Relations, a position of great prestige and horrible back-home political vulnerability. The last two senators who had chaired Foreign Relations had lost for re-election, victims of voters who punished them for spending too much time in Paris. *Mais oui.*

Bill Strauss had been working for Senator Percy for a little over a year, when Percy asked Bill to be counsel and staff director of the subcommittee and organize a staff of eight.

Per our title, we had three somewhat disjointed responsibilities—energy policy, the global spread of nukes, and anything at all having to do with government bureaucracy. Senator Percy used our subcommittee to focus on four areas of personal interest: Illinois, energy conservation (which he was for, especially in Illinois), nuclear proliferation (which he was against, including in Illinois), and government waste (which he was against, except in Illinois).

Some subcommittees carried weight and reputation, as investigative arms with subpoena powers, or were so busy writing "superfranticun-productivenothinglegislation" that their staffs were incredibly stressed out all the time. Not us. In between trips to Illinois, and our many hearings, we had a little spare time for a little good time, using our allotted personnel, budget, and office space to organize a softball team and a political comedy troupe.

This latter task began on a sunny Sunday in June 1981, on the same weekend Israeli warplanes were bombing Saddam Hussein's partly built nuclear reactor. That's when Bill hosted a party for the committee and personal staffs of Senator Percy, save those who had to man the hotlines to the Middle East. Some of the people who came to that party, especially guitarist Chris Manion, an aide to Percy nemesis Jesse Helms, knew something about music too.

After the party, Chris and a few other stragglers lingered in Bill's loft. Out of nowhere, we began jamming some parody lyrics to "Battle of New Orleans." To wit: "In 1980, the Senate took a flip... / We all kept score, and the Democrats were runnin' / There wasn't nigh as many as there was a while ago...And all they got was Gavin for the post of Mexico." And then there was (to "Me and Bobby McGee"): "Lefever's just another word for nothin' left to lose."

Well, it *seemed* funny at the time.

Nothing came of that for three summer months—during which the U.S. Capitol broiled with funny jokes about Ron and Nancy Reagan, Ed Meese, James Watt, and various other *notarati novi*. Meanwhile, we went back to the tedium of our daily lives running hearings to promote life, liberty, the pursuit of happiness, and the reelection of our senator.

In those days, Congressional offices were crowded but fun, full of airborne caffeine and bustling interns—a word which then had exciting, even uplifting connotations. Capitol Hill was (and still is) a place where, with deft and maneuver, a thirty-year-old could turn an entire cabinet agency upside down. All you had to do was get two minutes with your senator, get him to agree with the gist of what you wanted to do, put a hearing on his schedule (often the hardest part), and secure the use of his autopen signature to demand that witnesses show up. Love that autopen.

A Congressional hearing is like a high school play, except with worse microphones. You don't exactly know how it's going to go, but you desperately want to fill the room with attentive guests with cameras, and you spend a lot of time making nice props and sets, so no one will notice if the performers flub their lines.

Our subcommittee swiftly became notorious for energetic use of oversize props—charts, photos, giant Treasury checks—anything to create buzz, urgency, and TV appeal. We always tried to find some clever gimmick to get press.

Usually, we lured enough reporters and cameras in the room to please our chairman, to attract other senators to drop by, and to help us build a track record that helped us get quality witnesses for later hearings.

What we did in those hearings—as anyone actually present could surmise—was provide political entertainment—what Jay Leno once called "show biz for ugly people."

Gradually, we came upon a discovery: if B-grade actors (like Reagan) could become politicians, then B-grade politicians (like us) could become actors.

We feel obliged, at this point, to state for the record that our subcommittee conducted every single one of Charles Percy's hearings with the full measure of duty, dignity, decorum, and decency owed to the fine people of Illinois, whom we were so capably assisting him in representing. (And we have Memorial Bridge we'd like to sell you.) In truth, we actually were quite a busy subcommittee. We're proud of what we accomplished on the serious side, and we think the taxpayers got fair value from our meager paychecks.

TRACK: 3

★★★★★★★★★★★★★★★★

**Hark When Gerald Ford Was King
(parody of
"Hark the Herald Angels Sing")**

Hark when Gerald Ford was king
We were bored with everything
Unemployment, six percent
What a boring president
Nothin' major needed fixin'
So he pardoned Richard Nixon
Public anger he incurred
Carter and Reagan, we preferred
Now, with Ronald Reagan king
No one is bored with anything

But enough disclaimers: Exactly *what is it* that makes the Congress so funny?

The one hundred senators and 435 congresspeople are indeed what they claim to be: true representatives of the American people. They've got every foible in our national fable. The seven deadly sins? The voters got 'em, and so do the people they elect. Think of Congress as the dorky student body president you remember from middle school, all grown up, times 535. Imagine how funny your friends and neighbors would be if they had no specific work they had to do, sixty staffers on their payroll, easy access to reporters, and hundreds of thousands of dollars to spend on negative ads against anybody who tries to take their job away.

Congressmen and senators like the world to think they lead lives just like the rest of us—sure, like riding in elevators that the rest of us can't ride in, knowing for certain they'll have a place to park when they get to an airport, mailing hundreds of thousands of letters for free, flying to golf holidays on military jets, always having gladhands telling them how smart and wonderful they are—real everyday-people kinds of things.

Yes, congressmen and senators put their pants on one leg at a time. It's just that some of them take their pants off, also one leg at a time, a little more often than they should.

Inspired by these 535 individuals, Bill spent the summer of 1981 completing those half-baked, half-written songs that the Percy crew had jammed up in his loft, that June night. He'd never before been on stage, apart from a third-rate role in a second grade play, but odd showbizzy fantasies were entering his brain. Then, in one of those Bonnie-meets-Clyde, Laurel-meets-Hardy moments, Bill discovered to his amazement that the star pitcher of his subcommittee softball team, the writer of multiple monumental memos, a young woman he had hired a few months earlier, had been a music major at the University of Maryland—and played a mean piano. We speak, of course, of Elaina. The rest is herstory.

Three others in adjacent offices (Nancy Baskin, Barbie Granzow, and Dave Nichols) could actually hold a tune, and another (Jim Aidala) knew something about microphones and sound systems. Dave and Jim were on the subcommittee staff. Nancy was a legislative correspondent, writing answers to all the "Dear Chuck" letters senators received in those

  SIXTEEN SCANDALS

pre-anthrax days. Barbie was a secretary in another Percy office. We'd all gotten to know each other through the Percy softball team's many triumphs.

Through the summer and early fall, Bill passed around some goofball lyrics, Elaina and the others added some ideas of their own, and suddenly the thought arose: *Hey, let's put on a show.*

If it sounds like an old Andy Hardy movie, with Mickey Rooney and Judy Garland trying to put on a swell show in some old barn, well, it sorta kinda maybe *was.*

At first, we thought about putting on a traditional nativity play. But throughout the entire Congress, we couldn't find three wise men or a virgin.

We made the decision to put on more than a skit, more than your average Christmas show. At one rehearsal, somebody said, "Don't you think we're going overboard here?"—but the rest of us wanted to press on, so we did.

Through October and November, while President Reagan was merrily proposing MX missiles and B-1 bombers, we rehearsed. Yes, we rehearsed more for that silly Christmas show than for any show since, including our four New York off-Broadway openings.

We needed a name. We thought briefly about the Washington Maul (too malevolent, we agreed), and then Elaina recalled the Jenrette episode. The Capitol Steps. Yeah. That works.

We typed up and reproduced a few dozen programs emblazoned with "Capitol Steps" on the cover—with a clumsy little logo (the first of three over the years)—a song list inside, and enough apologias and thank you's to protect our collective derrieres if Anybody Important perchance got offended.

On Friday, December 11, 1981, on the very same day that Argentina's civilian president was sacked by a military junta, the six of us put on the very first Capitol Steps show, a Christmas party for the Foreign Relations Committee. We sang nine songs, some about the

★★★★★★★★★★★★★★★

16 Funniest Political Scandals, Since 1980

1. Bill Clinton and Monica Lewinsky
2. Ollie North and Iran-Contra
3. Bob Packwood's groping
4. Gary Hart's *Monkey Business*
5. Bill Clinton and Paula Jones
6. Marion Barry's drug bust
7. Clarence Thomas and Anita Hill
8. Tailhook
9. Newt Gingrich's ethics violations
10. The Clinton pardons
11. Dick Morris's toe-sucking
12. Army's Aberdeen Proving Grounds
13. Gary Condit
14. Whitewater
15. Jim Wright's book deal
16. Jenrettes trysting on the Capitol steps

Senate, but most about Reagan. ("I fit the proper pattern of a pure and princely president / Plainly in the White House I'm a perfect present res- ident," to the tune of Gilbert and Sullivan's "I Am the Very Model of a Modern Major General.")

Some of our lyrics were funny, and some (we admit) were not. The audience was astonished, less by the quality of our singing or joke-telling than by our sheer audacity at having attempted this. Over the years, people have often asked us whether we thought our silly little Christmas show would ever lead to a professional act, numerous TV and radio spe- cials, and twenty-two record albums. The answer, most definitely, is no.

Halfway through the show, around the fourth or fifth song, a young Senate staffer breathlessly rushed into the anteroom we'd been using as a backstage. Face reddening, body heaving, arms waving, the young staffer ordered us to stop the show.

"Why?" we asked.

"Senator Pell is coming."

"No," we told her. "The show must go on." And it has, through twenty years, sixteen scandals, and who knows how many laughs.

SIXTEEN SCANDALS

2

Quoth the Reagan,
"Cut Some More"
("Make My Ketchup a Vegetable")

★★★★★★★★★
TRACKS: 4–5

To our surprise and delight, official Washington took a liking to our silly little Christmas show. Taking the advice of assorted friends, we kept it up and running. That first December of 1981, we performed those nine songs nine times, becoming—as Jim Aidala liked to say—the U.S. Senate's new "tap-dancing cat." Hauling props around in huge multicolored canvas bags, we performed in hallways, foyers, journalists' living rooms, Christmas parties where nobody paid the slightest attention because everybody was too busy networking (or drinking). We capped off that first month with our first public show, a nicely attended event in an ornate Capitol anteroom just off the Senate Floor.

★★★★★★★★★★★★★★★★

**Mutual Annihilation Society
(parody of
"Mutual Admiration Society")**

We belong to a mutual annihilation society
Ronnie and me
We belong to a mutua-a-a-al annihilation
    society
You're building weapons by the score
There's room for many many more
I'll cut back one, you cut back two
Please, after you
No, after you
I'll do exactly what I'd like
I think he's planning a first strike
He has the means to blow me into
    smithereens

The Capitol Steps had become a very minor media sensation, with reporters from various national networks and large papers struck less by our creativity than by our bravery in risking our jobs by persisting in making fun of our bosses. Questions from the press made us nervous. That first December, an ABC producer asked us if we wanted to go on *Nightline* or *Good Morning America*, and we said thank you, no. We asked her and other reporters to keep a lid on our show, since it *was* true, we *were* risking our jobs, and one nasty story in a major paper could have not only stopped our show, it could have made us unemployable in Reagan-era Washington. (We were Republicans, remember.)

As the Christmas party era ended and the new year broke, we began wondering: maybe we should let go of this, while we were still safe and secure in our jobs. But it was too much fun—and, like everyone else in Congress, we just didn't know when to stop. If one show was good, ten shows would be outstanding, and a hundred shows would be delirium. The deficit was growing from week to week, so why not the Capitol Steps? The reporters laughed, winked, and kept us out of the public eye, as we asked. Meanwhile, we forged on with our double lives—staffers by day, comics by night.

We expanded our cast to include people from the House, some of them Democrats, including the witty Alan Friedman, who came with several very funny song ideas. Through 1982, we added several others who can be heard on our first album, which wasn't to come for two more years. We performed with a cast as large as ten, twice the size of our current show. By June 1982, fewer than half of the Capitol Steps came from our subcommittee staff, but we were still widely perceived as a Percy operation.

As we got rolling, much of our comic point of view came from our senatorial work. We featured Interior Secretary James Watt as a witness in a hearing about his plans to "streamline" (translation: privatize) federal lands management, and then roasted him in a take-off of *The Sound*

of Music's "Climb Ev'ry Mountain." ("Mine ev'ry mountain / Fill ev'ry stream / Level ev'ry hillside / 'Til you find your seam.")

We held tedious oversight hearings into plans to pare back low-income energy assistance programs of the Energy Department, after which we lampooned Edgar Allan Poe's "The Raven." ("Deep in my department dreary / While I labored weak and weary / On some memorandum bleary / And some other office chore / Suddenly I heard a cutting / Like the sound of scissors shutting / Then I knew someone was gutting / Gutting programs for the poor / Quoth the Reagan / 'Cut some more.'")

We investigated overspending by defense contractors, after which we rewrote the *Oliver* ballad, "Who Will Buy My Sweet Red Roses?" as "Who will buy my brand new hammer / For ten thousand dollars?"

We had extensive hearings on weapons proliferation and followed them up with a song about Argentina's previously secret plans to join the nuclear club. ("Don't build the bomb Argentina… / If you show ill will / You know Brazil will.")

We investigated the U.S. nuclear weapons supply chain, and wrote a parody of "Old Man River" about "Old Clinch River," a breeder reactor that "just keeps rollin' along." The realpolitik of that one utterly exasperated us. ("You ask why hasn't it met its maker / It's represented by Howard Baker.")

The night after the U.S. Senate killed the Clinch River Breeder Reactor by just one vote—Senator Percy's—we celebrated professionally (and mourned comedically) by singing the song one last time, wearing black arm bands.

We also had a lot of songs about global issues in those days, befitting the Foreign Relations chairmanship of Senator Percy. The arms race was heating up, the Reagan tax cuts for the rich were miraculously trickling down to fund a major new U.S. nuclear weapons buildup. "On what must Congress spend the nation's wealth?" the Reagan in our show asked, in a parody of "Rain in Spain." The answer: "Immense expense is mainly in defense"—illustrated by a huge dollar sign and green check that we had in fact used in one of our subcommittee hearings on defense waste.

In those years, the pre-*perestroika* Soviet Union was spending its way into bankruptcy, matching us bomb for bomb in what we described in song as a "mutual annihilation society." Americans were a little scared by it all, understandably, but that little edge of fear helped audiences to laugh at our songs.

We felt, in our wicked and warped way, that through our show, as in our subcommittee hearings, we could provide a little check and balance to the various wrongs we saw in the world. When people laughed, that meant they were connecting, that our point had landed, and we were pleased by that.

Every one of the above—Watt's lands sell-off, the energy cuts, Argentina's nuclear program, defense contractor waste, the Clinch River Breeder Reactor, even (years later) the U.S.–Soviet arms race—was slowed and, eventually, stopped cold.

We didn't think about it at the time—mainly, we were just having a little fun, trying to deliver a little message wrapped in a joke (or was it the other way around?) while avoiding getting our names in the papers—but we were inadvertently stepping into a long and proud American tradition: using humor to hold leaders accountable.

Satire is at least as old as Hellenic plays and has existed in many centuries and cultures, but the modern American genre derives from *Mother Goose*, anti-crown ditties a commoner could sing without too much fear of being hanged. The tradition came to the New World colonies, but not with the first settlers. In no history book does it say that the Puritans left England to live where they could loosen up and get a good laugh—more the opposite. With the likes of John Winthrop, Cotton Mather, Jonathan Edwards, those first two colonial centuries were grimly sober. No one dared tell jokes or publish satires about the Salem witch trials in their own time.

The eighteenth century brought Jonathan Swift's *Gulliver's Travels*, Voltaire's *Candide,* and a new so-called Age of Enlightenment. Early stirrings of a new American sense of humor can be seen in Benjamin Franklin's *Poor Richard's Almanac.* By the 1760s, the "Don't Tread on Me" flags with coiled snakes and the loud shouts of liberty revealed sharper tongues than had theretofore been heard in the colonies.

The Revolution itself delivered yet more rambunctious spirit, as wars seem to do, as a way of releasing the tensions people feel when being swept up in epic historical moments. Jokes abounded about King

George III, colonial governors, and Parliament. Amid the fervid Patrick Henrys and Tom Paines, and the analytical Jeffersons and Madisons, a new sense of humor began to emerge with old Ben Franklin's homilies, tweaks, pinches, and winks at the ladies. Sexual mores were loosening up a bit in the late eighteenth century, and the jokes—and satire—began to flow in a new and distinctly American vein.

American patriots still stole their melodies from Mother England, but they began making fun of their own leaders—George Washington excepted. During the Revolutionary War, insults in song and joke were shouted back and forth across battle lines where, if you were close enough to shoot to kill, you were close enough to yell at your target. Amid blasts of gunpowder, a favorite chant for combatants of both sides was to parody the English ditty "Lucy Locket."

All Americans know the anti-royalist verse, "Yankee Doodle went to London / Riding on a pony / Stuck a feather in his cap / And called it macaroni." Among its many variations was a call to arms, "Sing Yankee Doodle, that fine tune / Americans delight in / It suits for fun / It suits as well for fightin'." More than a decade later, following the French Revolution of 1789, Doodle turned against the French and their American Jacobin sympathizers: "Yankee Doodle, mind the tune / Yankee Doodle dandy / If Frenchmen come with naked bum / We'll spank 'em hard and handy."

In the new American nation, the satirical barbs remained sharp in the feuds between Federalists and their Jeffersonian adversaries. The unbeloved John Adams got roasted with "See Johnny at the helm of state / Head itching for a crowny / He longs to be, like Georgy, great / And pull Tom Jeffer Downy," to which the Federalists responded with a parody of "God Save the Queen": "'Tis the wretches who wait / To unite church and state / The name of our Jefferson ever to hate."

Starting in the 1790s, an English drinking tune—"To Anacreon in Heaven"—became an especially popular tune for political messages, sometimes funny, other times purely adversarial. Two decades later, Francis Scott Key attached a more earnest poem to that same melody, known then and since as "The Star-Spangled Banner." Not every War of 1812 parody was quite so patriotic: "That horrid war we used to hate / We love it dearly now / We never talked of bloody graves / Dang it anyhow."

The Jacksonian era produced more populist humor, and the Congress now came under withering assault ("These hardy knaves and stupid fools / Some apish and pragmatic mules / Some servile acquiescing fools / These, these, compose the Congress"). The Corrupt Bargain election of 1824, perhaps the most overtly crooked in our history, got mocked in song: "With hearts turned to rapture, let's hail this bright day / Beneath the bland influence of Adams and Clay."

Americans didn't have nearly as many popular tunes then as we do now, but whatever songs our ancestors knew, they butchered to make political points. The "singing campaign" of 1840 may have been our most musical presidential race ever. The Whigs and Democrats didn't have polls or focus groups—lucky them—so they gauged their support by the musical noise their supporters could produce while marching down the street. The fans of "Tippecanoe and Tyler Too" tunefully derided Martin Van Buren as stupid, bald, small, and weak. ("Old Tip he wears a homespun coat / He has no ruffled shirt-wirt-wirt / But Mat he has the golden plate / And he's a little squirt-wirt-wirt.") The Whigs made the "wirt" sound by spitting through their teeth, often lubricated by tobacco. On one occasion, sixty thousand whigs marched from Boston Common to Bunker Hill chanting this song and "wirting" along the muddy roadside.

The music and humor grew meaner into the 1850s, with the "Lincoln Shouters" and "Hurrah Boys" gibing at the "Know Nothings," "Southrons," and others, who often chanted right back. But as the storm of secession gathered, joking gave way to violence.

In the Civil War, the guns were more powerful than during the Revolution, so the warring sides didn't sing at each other, but they butchered plenty of songs between their bloody bouts. These songs dwelt more on steel and eternal damnation than on the funny quirks of whoever was pillaging and burning the farms in the vicinity. "The Battle Hymn of the Republic" was a parody of a minstrel song, and its stern lyrics grew tougher as the years passed and casualties mounted ("We'll hang Jeff Davis from a sour apple tree…"). Meanwhile, both sides—North and South—claimed the song "Dixie" as their own.

At the end of the war, any thought of a lifting mood, and return to old-style American musical politics, gave way to the grim mood that

followed Lincoln's assassination. Blues replaced ballads, and wordless Sousa-style military marches became popular. Satire disappeared from song almost completely—by now replaced by a new genre of political commentary, the editorial cartoon. By the 1880s, fresh stirrings arose, driven by the exciting new operettas of Gilbert and Sullivan, as in this chide of Democrats. ("As a white cadet, I made such a name / That a pet of the South I soon became / I wore white gloves and a bran' new suit / At the bottom of my class at the Institute.")

In the era bracketed by the 1890s and 1920s, America had some truly funny presidents, with numerous misdeeds in the mirth making realms of sex, money, and favor-trading deal-making. From Grover Cleveland ("Ma, ma / Where's your pa? / Up in the White House / Ha ha ha") to Warren Harding, with his famous tryst in the White House closet, plus the likes of the prim chum of business McKinley, Rough and Ready Teddy Roosevelt, three-hundred-pound Taft, the vainglorious and professorial Wilson, silent Cal, and the star-crossed "Hoobert Heever," everyone was fair game. In a newly raucous society, unionists, populists, feminists, prohibitionists, and other "ist-ers" used political barbs—often laced in songs—to skewer opponents and advance their various causes.

From Joe Hill's "Wobblies"—the radical labor songsters who fashioned parody into a tool of discontent—to H.L. Mencken's media lampooning of the "booboisie," political humor had a ring of class conflict. In the 1930s, this ripened into the downhome sketches of Will Rogers and songs of Woody Guthrie. The double-dose *gravitas* of the New Deal and World War II rendered the U.S. government less amusing than before, and the oversize personality of "That Man," Franklin Delano Roosevelt, became the main humor magnet, but seldom in song. The 1936 G.O.P. convention that nominated Alf Landon in 1936 reportedly included over a hundred parody verses of "O My Darling Clementine." Musical satire had reached a point of exhaustion. In wartime, the only

★★★★★★★★★★★★★★★★★
16 Funniest Scandals, U.S. History
1. Bill Clinton and Monica Lewinsky
2. Watergate
3. The Bobbitts
4. John Kennedy, Fiddle, and Faddle
5. Warren Harding's "girl in a closet"
6. Iran-Contra
7. O.J. Simpson trial
8. Victoria Woodhull's Free Love Party
9. Bob Packwood's groping
10. J. Edgar Hoover's secret love life
11. King George III's insanity
12. Grover Cleveland's bastard child
13. Gary Hart's *Monkey Business*
14. Thomas Jefferson and Sally Hemmings
15. Enron
16. Fatty Arbuckle trial

funny songs about "government issue" people were about the real "G.I.s"—soldiers.

Come the postwar years, the songs of Tom Lehrer and Stan Freberg, and the cartoons of *The New Yorker* and *Mad Magazine* offered slyly subversive commentary on the 1950 social scene, but seldom singed President Eisenhower. The '50s were culturally conformist partly because America felt so triumphant, but also because creative people felt a little uncomfortable about expressing a point of view. Joe McCarthy's red-baiting provided what today would be a comedic cornucopia, but it sure didn't seem so at the time. Very few people made light of anyone who could glibly publish lists of supposed leftists and thereby ruin careers of people in the entertainment business. In those days of the House UnAmerican Activities Committee, nearly no one publicly joked about the Congress. The new TV comedy shows bristled with brilliant writers and performers (Steve Allen, Sid Caesar, Lucille Ball, Jackie Gleason, Red Skelton, Ernie Kovacs) who, were they alive today, would probably include at least something political, but not then.

John Kennedy may have catalyzed a newly creative era, but that creativity seldom extended to comedic mirrors on his own Camelot. In hindsight, his could (and perhaps should) have been a scandal-a-month presidency. What could be more amusing than a president going one-on-one with movie stars, or having affairs with babes with mafiosi and spy connections, or skinny-dipping in the White House pool with secretaries code-named Fiddle and Faddle? With the birth control pill just then being marketed, America remained on the eve of a so-called "sexual revolution." As the press curiously conspired to conceal Kennedy's peccadilloes, Americans of both genders and all ideological ilks were expected to ignore (perhaps even admire) this kind of behavior, not laugh at it.

A month after Vaughn Meader presented a tamely affectionate comedic take on the Kennedy "First Family," Lee Harvey Oswald stripped away whatever new interest may have been developing in making jokes about U.S. presidents. In 1964, the very clever *That Was the Week That Was* bucked that trend, but only briefly—its cancellation reflecting the growing sense that outrage now had to accompany satire.

If you weren't there, the 1960s were perhaps the funniest modern decade—listen to today's teens howl at *Austin Powers* if you doubt that—but those of us who lived through those creative but anger-laden times can seldom recall hearing laugh-out-loud jokes about political issues. The funniest people, in hindsight, were the Beatles—imports—and when they started getting political, they stopped being funny. Everything felt too serious to joke about—the war, the draft, poverty, race, women's issues, even the culture.

It wasn't easy to tell a bipartisan joke about the Chappaquiddick scandal, young Senator Ted Kennedy's tragic weekend fling with a young staffer—nor about Woodstock, Patty Hearst, Angela Davis, the Harvard riots, or any of the countless colorful events and personalities of those years. Taking cues from the Smothers Brothers and Tom Paxton, comic songsters took clear sides on issues—usually the same antiestablishment side. This orthodoxy may explain why, through the 1960s, no one launched a political cabaret in Washington, D.C.

On the brink of Watergate, Richard Nixon made a brief but memorable appearance on Dan Rowan and Dick Martin's *Laugh-In*, several comedians (notably Richard Little) began rendering pretty fair impressions of him, and Mark Russell offered his *Sing a Song of Watergate* album and show, but once the scandal reached fervor proportions, the case became so severe, and the threats against Nixon's presidency so decisive, that nothing seemed all that funny.

Post-Watergate presidential humor returned with Gerald Ford, in a new slapstick genre akin to the national mood of relief. Chevy Chase of vintage *Saturday Night Live* made Ford's physical pratfalls a source of national fun. In a new twist, the warm-hearted Ford often joined in the joke, helping cement an image of clumsiness that would oddly stick to a president who may have been the most athletic in our history. In Ford's close reelection loss to Carter, the accumulated public memory of Chevy Chase's head bumps sure didn't help. That 1976 election campaign, with its jokes about "WIN" buttons, Poland, and other "gaffes" (a newly popular word), may have been the first in which late-night comic monologues helped average Americans get their political news.

Meanwhile, our own baby boom generation was coming of age with our own point of view—on the whole, a far more sarcastic, iconoclastic attitude than our predecessors had shown. We were risk-takers, edgy, a little nasty even, having pushed up every negative statistic of adolescence

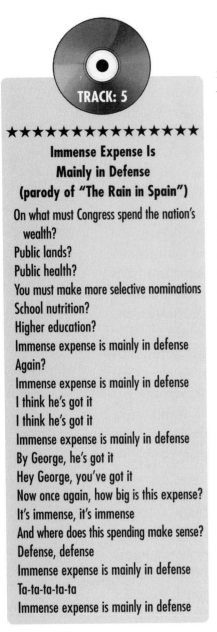
from crime to drugs to teen pregnancy, even as we were pushing average SAT scores down.

Having grown up sneaking peeks at *Playboy* cartoons, we Americans then in their twenties and thirties felt far more at ease with overtly sexual humor than our parents had ever been. Among those of us who had been in high school or college during the '60s and early '70s, there was this cocky sense that sure, our parents procreated us, but they didn't have nearly enough fun doing it. Maybe our generation hadn't actually *invented* sex, but we were certainly hard at work testing it, perfecting it, dissecting it, and making jokes about it in ways older people couldn't fathom.

We also had an inclination, and opportunity, for parodies. That resulted partly from our left-brain bent, partly from our defiance of legal huffings and puffings, but mostly from the vast talents of those who made the music of those two culturally creative decades. There may be no generation in U.S. history that can match the boomers' devotion to and pride in their coming-of-age pop music. Back in those eighteenth and nineteenth centuries, song parodists had little more than Stephen Foster, church hymnals, and assorted children's and drinking songs, but boomers had Bob Dylan, Simon and Garfunkel, the Beatles, Beach Boys, Bee Gees, you name it—plus decades of show tunes, Sinatra croons, and more. In the early '80s, what people today chide as dinosaur rock felt incredibly fresh, and, with few exceptions, no one had ever parodied those tunes.

Our generation had some other satirical advantages, too. From the 1790s through the 1840s, political people wrote and sang political parodies, and other barbs, about rakish drunks, Whigs in wigs, backwoods populists who tracked dirty boots through the White House, and others who resembled our A-list of targets. Except they had spittoons and we didn't—and we had bureaucrats and they didn't. In the two centuries since then, the government has grown aplenty, and the jokes have grown apace.

Finding our first authentic comedic voice after Watergate, with the vintage cast of *Saturday Night Live*, our generation looked upon everything as fair target. We assumed we would not just change the world (that, we assumed, would be easy), but—maybe more important—we would also bring our fresh, irreverent style.

Which is exactly what we intended to do, in those early days of the Capitol Steps. After we'd spent about a year in our work-by-day, comedy-by-night double life—we were then doing two to four shows a month—our subcommittee developed a bit of a reputation around Washington. We would go to some meeting, in advance of a hearing, in some windowless room off some barren corridor on some vast floor in some nondescript building where we'd sit in some lumpy chairs around some chipped-veneer table, trying to press some gray-suited bureaucrats into admitting they'd been wasting the taxpayers' hard-earned money, only to have our hosts freeze in mid-discussion, peer at us, lean forward, and ask, "Hey, aren't *you* the Capitol Steps?"

We'd admit that, yes, we were, but that we also had real jobs to do, after which they'd often ask us, half in jest, whether we were there looking for material. For awhile, we'd answer that question "no," but eventually we learned that a "maybe" answer could be useful. When they heard that, and realized that we weren't joking, they took us far more seriously than before.

Comedy, as part of a free and vibrant press, serves as a check and balance on the excesses of power. That's a clear lesson of history. And as the Capitol Steps did more shows before larger audiences, we began learning our part of that lesson. If we wanted to do our show before people who would actually pay money to see it, we had to take some chances, to give our show a little more bite.

If it fell to us to carry the torch of Yankee Doodle, it also fell to us to move beyond the issues we worked on, as Senate staffers, and take after President Reagan more directly, whenever he pulled a feather from his cap and called it macaroni.

Within a few weeks after our show began, the Reagan Administration declared ketchup to qualify as a "vegetable" required by Congress to be in federally subsidized school lunches. Parodying "Herod's Song" from *Jesus Christ Superstar*, we sang, "Prove to me that you're so able / Make my ketchup a vegetable." Big laugh. Before long, ketchup was out of the veggie bin, back on the condiment shelf.

Maybe this was "the Teflon Presidency," as the press often complained, but the jokes stuck solidly to the frying pan. And the president laughed at them, too.

Dutch the Magic Reagan ("Workin' 9 to 10")

★★★★★★★★★
TRACKS: 6–9

"You're all under arrest."

We'd just finished the show of our dreams, a show for the ages, on the southern portico of the White House, through a warm early September twilight, before an audience of three hundred that included half the Congress, much of the Cabinet, and our hosts, President and Mrs. Ronald Reagan. It had taken us seven years, but we got there.

Before we performed, the president had instructed us, through an aide, to make fun not of Democrats, senators, or congressmen, only of him. So we did. We opened the show with a parody of "Workin' 9 to 5," featuring Bill Strauss as Reagan, singing lyrics

TRACK: 6

★★★★★★★★★★★★★★★★
Get Me to the Dirge on Time
(parody of
"Get Me to the Church on Time")

REAGAN
Each time a nation is in mourning
My own invitation I decline
Asian or Russian
I'm sending Bush in
I send him to the dirge each time
BUSH
Who's getting buried in the morning?
Moscow in winter is sublime
I travel often to pass by a coffin
I'm always at the dirge
REAGAN
On flowers you will splurge
Ol' George is always at the dirge on time

that would have gotten him shot in other latitudes and longitudes: "Nine A.M., my blood's not pumpin' / Wonder which staffers Nancy's been dumpin' / Check the watch, thank God I'm almost done / Workin' 9 to 10, puttin' total effort in it / That's my regimen, sixty solid workin' minutes / As your president, I won't cut that any smaller / 'Cuz I get free rent and two hundred thousand dollars."

While Bill sang, he looked at the first lady, who stared and glared, and then at Reagan, who laughed and laughed—along with the hundreds of members of Congress present, who knew the core joke about this president was how hard he was (*not?*) working, how much sleep (*during meetings?*) he was getting, and how many working (*on horseback?*) vacations he took at his beloved ranch in the Santa Barbara mountains. Reagan had once quipped that he refused to become the first U.S. president to die from overwork. Whether you liked Reagan or not, and whatever you thought of his presidency, you had to admit he had a brilliant entertainer's instinct for knowing how to stay a step ahead of comedians—not to mention those who tried to ridicule him as a way of diminishing him.

When the president-to-be revealed a light touch in his debates against Jimmy Carter—and especially when, in March 1981, the new president joked with his doctors while he still had Hinckley's bullet lodged in his chest—this gave the rest of us permission to laugh, too.

We knew that we wouldn't be doing him, the presidency, or the Republic, any harm by making a few jokes at his expense. Lyndon Johnson and Richard Nixon had famously stewed over public and personal criticisms, down to the way their faces were drawn by political cartoonists, but Reagan just seemed to laugh it off, mainly by telling his own jokes about how he was a man of simple tastes and simpler truths who never under any circumstances changed his mind about anything, no matter how many experts were lined up against him—and a man who would always save a smile and handshake for his adversaries.

Reagan was our first true "talking head" president, and he was good at that, but he was at his best and wittiest self on the stump, where he mixed his serious simple messages with self-effacing humor. Part of the reason this worked with audiences, and what we tried to convey in our show, was the palpable sense of relief Americans felt that perhaps all the Vietnam-Watergate-Stagflation-Malaise-era talk of national decline might come to an end. Jokes you make about a national up-tick are very different from jokes about a down-tick, and even though America was in a recession in the early '80s, it sure felt like an up-tick.

We presented an effervescent, optimistic Reagan who believed in very basic things, and was a tad confused by all the fuss and bother those beliefs were creating. First Lady Nancy was yang to that yin. But when Nancy appeared onstage at the spring 1982 gridiron dinner, singing a parody of "Second Hand Rose" about her "second-hand clothes"—she of the tip-to-toe designer cloth—the first lady succeeded in charming the media, temporarily restricting the comic take on her to matters of style more than personality.

★★★★★★★★★★★★★★★★
**16 Funniest Non-Scandals,
U.S. History**

1. Vice President Dan Quayle
2. Operation Desert Storm
3. McCarthy hearings
4. Y2K election
5. Prohibition and the mob
6. Woodstock
7. Political correctness
8. Spanish-American War
9. "Dewey Beats Truman"
10. Aging baby boomers
11. Cold War arms race
12. Muckraking
13. Robber barons
14. War of 1812
15. Reaganomics
16. Whiskey Rebellion

When the public has a clear perception of the leading characters and issues, this makes the satirist's job easier. If the leaders and their stands are controversial—which they most definitely were in those years—so much the better. In those heady days of first-term Reagamania, when it was OK to run deficits, to cut taxes for the rich, to build missiles, and to strip mine, it was also OK to laugh about all that. The issues were clear-cut, the personalities bold and colorful. People connected at a gut level, whether they agreed or not.

Everyone knew the Reagan agenda—an agenda so basic we could translate it into Latin in our ersatz Christmas carol, "O Come Reagan Faithful," *Adeste Fidelis*: *"Arreste Nudilis / Bi Te Demo Cratis / Veni Vidi Vici / Vacintan / No Benefitum / Exceptum Tru Li Nidium / De Crisium De Spendium / De Crisium De Taxum / In Crisium De Fensum / Ranius."*

★★★★★★★★★★★★★★★★

Workin' 9 to 10
(parody of "Workin' 9 to 5")

REAGAN

Workin' every day in the Oval Office
Thinkin' up anecdotes and sophistries
My workin' day has just begun
Nine AM, my blood's not pumpin'
Wonder which staffers Nancy's been
 dumpin'
Check the watch, thank God I'm almost
 done
Workin' nine to ten
Puttin' total effort in it
That's my regimen
Sixty solid workin' minutes as your
President
I won't cut that any smaller
I get free rent and two hundred thousand
 dollars

Spendum, Taxum, De Fensum: those were the cornerstones of Reaganomics, that miracle elixir the president rammed down everybody's throats to dig this country out of the early '80s recession and enrich a few thousand of his dearest dining companions.

The Reagan plan was so childlike in its simplicity that we chose children's songs to chide it. To the tune of "Puff the Magic Dragon," we sang "Dutch the Magic Reagan / Helped us to see / The meaning of the magic of / Supply-side policy." We brought a frizzy-wigged Little Orphan Annie onstage to sing "My budget will be elastic / Never pay with cash when you have plastic / From today / I'll borrow / I'll borrow / I'll mortgage tomorrow / And pay back another day."

When David Stockman quit and expressed his remorse in a tell-all article in the *Atlantic Monthly*, in which he called Reaganomics a "Trojan horse" for a long-term agenda of starving the U.S. government—the real Reagan "took him to the woodshed," but in this new Decade of Greed, Stockman got the last laugh by getting a huge advance to write a tell-all book, after which he made even more money working as an investment banker.

Reagan's budget director was not the only Reagan official to publish a high-profile book. So did Attorney General Edwin Meese, who proudly released an official Justice Department compendium on obscenity that no parent would dare show a child. We thought that exercise to be, well, just a little Mickey Mouse. So we donned mouse ears, held up big letter cards, and sang, "Come along and join the throng against pornography / led by E D Double-U I N, M E E S E / Say a dirty word and get a censorship decree / Straight from E D Double-U I N, M E E S E / Edwin Meese / Daffy duck / Edwin Meese / What rhymes with duck? / Pornography will lead us all to crime-crime-crime-crime."

With material like this, the Capitol Steps were merrily chugging along, doing shows wherever we could, nearly always for free, sometimes in shows where we outnumbered the audience, like at George

Washington Law School, where exactly two people came to see us. We had no microphones and often had to scream our songs to be heard. For props, Bill stole from his children's toy collection. Those were the days.

In the eyes of Washingtonians, we were the Office Party That Could Not Be Stopped. Other parties may have feasted on *canard l'orange* and six-inch shrimp, but we were proof positive of the virtues of a multi-party political system: one party goofs up, the other party parties, and the party of the fourth part makes fun of it all.

The early Reagan years rambled on with low-grade foibles, fluffy stuff, and far-off tragedies—Charles and Di's first baby, the coining of the word "yuppie," and a tunnel blast that killed hundreds of Russians in some irrelevant place called Afghanistan. No big scandals, but plenty of material for satire nonetheless.

Being Senate staffers leading a double life—still asking the press to keep us "off the record"—the Capitol Steps had a more immediate concern. Our boss, paymaster, and protector, Senator Charles Percy, was nearing the end of his third term and faced a conservative challenger in a primary election. This opponent, Tom Corcoran, was a congressman with a record for no-holds-barred campaigning. We suspected that he'd hesitate for oh, maybe ten or twenty seconds before pointing to how Percy's staff was out ridiculing President Reagan, proof positive why Percy should be drummed out of the Republican Party.

As the calendar turned ever closer to the primary election, we fully expected the senator to ask us to stop the silliness, at least for awhile. But he never did. Charles Percy later told us he felt that, by contributing to Washington's sense of humor, we were doing something important, hence he tolerated the risk that this whole thing might blow up in his face and ours. Even so, we took it upon ourselves to play it safe, pulling some punches we wouldn't have in later years.

Bill Strauss played Reagan straight-up, no wig, no mannerisms, nothing over the top, just a princely purple sash across his blue blazer. His goal was to project the inner Reagan, not the outer one, which we left to Jim Morris and other impressionists. Our Nancys (Nancy Baskin, Mary Joyce) also sang the role without affect, with nothing more than a "hi, Nancy" as introduction.

★★★★★★★★★★★★★★★

**Don't Know Much about
Who Fought Who
(parody of
"Don't Know Much about History")**

REPORTER
Welcome President Reagan
Come on, and tell the press
Why foreign trips you've taken
Always end up such an awful me-ess
REAGAN
Don't know much about history
Don't know much geography
Don't know much about World War II
Don't know much about who fought who
But I know it followed World War I
If we only fought in wars we won
What a wonderful world this would be
REPORTER
We know you're not an Abe Lincoln
Or Franklin Roosevelt
It's time we started thinking
What place in history will you be dea-ealt?
REAGAN
Don't know what's my place in history
What I'm leavin' for posterity
Don't know what biographers will tell
But they'll say I did one thing real well
I knew how to beat a Democrat
If my party could do more of that
What a wonderful world this would be

Our jokes were basic and studiously bipartisan. We were still mostly Republicans, but by now we had several Democrats too. For some shows, we marked a little *R* (for Republican) and *D* (for Democrat) next to each song, indicating which way it tilted, making sure we never leaned too far one way or the other. Too many *D*s, and we'd write a new *R* song. As it was, audiences usually thought we were all Democrats, perhaps because Reagan gibes remained the heart of the show.

In February 1983, fourteen months after our first show, the Marquee Lounge at the Shoreham Hotel—until a year earlier the home of Mark Russell—asked us if we'd like to do monthly shows on Monday nights. The room seated two hundred, the admission was three bucks, and we thought we didn't have a prayer of filling the place.

Now nightclub performers, we knew we had to let the media say what they might about our show. Roger Piantadosi of the *Washington Post* loved the show and gave us an A-plus review. The next several shows were packed, with lines out the door, and there wasn't a semicolon in his review that Tom Corcoran could use against Percy, or Percy's senior staff could use against us.

It's a legend of the entertainment business that your first main-paper review makes you or breaks you, and the Capitol Steps were no exception. We rode that *Post* review as far as we could. In the weeks that followed, we enjoyed some excellent press all over, in the *New York Times* and *Wall Street Journal*, followed in short order by clips on NBC and ABC evening news shows. We went from once a month on Mondays to twice a month on Fridays. We were on a roll.

"What's your goal?" the media kept asking. In truth, we didn't know what our goal was. It certainly wasn't to make a living at this (yet), since we still had our Senate jobs. To cover our bases, Elaina and Bill had an Official Capitol Steps Goal for Public Consumption: to perform in the White House for President Reagan.

We repeated that mantra often, when around prominent Republicans, especially Reagan's own aides. Conservatives didn't mind our show so much—they saw us as better-balanced than other wags.

Percy survived his primary challenge, but it left him vulnerable against a Democratic opponent, Paul Simon (the professor, not the songwriter). Again, we continued our show, again Senator Percy raised no objection, and again election day arrived without Illinois voters having the slightest inkling his staff was performing a political satire show in a prominent D.C. nightclub. Paul Simon knew about us—nearly every-one in the Congress did—but, like Tom Corcoran and the Illinois press, he left us alone and stuck to the real issues of the campaign.

In hindsight, we remain amazed that, through three years and well over a hundred shows, the Capitol Steps never made page 39D, much less the front page, of any newspaper in Illinois. If a troupe like ours were to start out today, in this era of campaign consultants, negative ads, and cable news, would they be treated as well? Maybe not. Politics was a little more civil then.

Senator Percy asked us to perform at his election night party in Chicago. We flew out to Illinois at our own expense, looking forward to a great show, no longer caring what the local press would say, except…Percy lost. Around the time we performed, everybody's nose was glued to the various TV screens, and no one was in a partying mood. Nor were we. When your senator loses, you're out of work.

That 1984 election year also saw Reagan trounce Walter "Fritz" Mondale, in a forty-eight-state landslide we chronicled in "The Wreck of the Walter Fritz Mondale" (apologies to "The Wreck of the Edmund Fitzgerald"). Just as Reagan's simplicity had worked for us as comedians, it worked for him in the polling place. In our takeoff of "Don't Know Much About History," our Reagan sang, "I know how to beat a

TRACK: 9

★★★★★★★★★★★★★★★★

**'Crats
(parody of "Memories")**

Election
And another rejection
And more voter defection
So we lost once again
What's become of
The Democratic party I love?
Only memories linger on

Democrat / If my party could do more of that / What a wonderful world this would be."

Audiences cheered. Little did they know that Bill and Elaina, the Capitol Steps cofounders, had lost their day jobs.

That's when we decided to go pro with the show. We agreed that, wherever we worked next, we'd cut a deal with our new bosses that would enable us to moonlight as paid political satirists. We recorded—and began selling—our first album, the only one with no joke in the title: *The Capitol Steps—Live! at the Shoreham.* We started doing occasional radio bits. Reporters called us up and asked for funny quotes, and we eagerly complied. We performed two songs for a live-to-tape national broadcast HBO special hosted by ex-President Ford in Grand Rapids, Michigan, on "Humor and the Presidency."

Our stated goal remained, as it had always been, to perform at the White House for President Reagan. In 1988, on that glorious September evening, we at long last got that chance—and, in the meantime, we had laid the groundwork for becoming a commercially viable act.

None of us could have imagined it. A bunch of Congressional staffers do a Christmas show, and end up as the first long-running political satire troupe in American history, poking fun at the same people who once had signed our paychecks.

4

Thank God I'm a Contra Boy ("We'll Do What Ollie Would")

★★★★★★★★
TRACKS: 10–12

In our early shows, our Reagan and his Soviet counterpart (Leonid Brezhnev) hoisted large gray foam-rubber cylinders that were supposed to be missiles but looked more like crayons. During one song, those two Cold War adversaries bopped each other over the head with them, to the delight of the audience—including, on one occasion, high-ranking officials from the Soviet Embassy, who called us soon afterwards with a luncheon invitation.

When we showed up, we encountered two men in bad suits and worse haircuts, only one of whom spoke passable English. His name was Viktor—with a "k," he made quite clear. He invited us to bring our show to Moscow. For a moment, we had visions of ending the

TRACK: 10

★★★★★★★★★★★★★★★

**While Reagan Sleeps Tonight
(parody of "The Lion Sleeps")**

Ee-e-e-e, e-e-e-e, e
Sandinistas on the way
Ee-e-e-e, e-e-e-e, e
Sandinistas on the way
In the jungle, there's been a bungle
While Reagan sleeps tonight
In Honduras, some army tourists
Have gotten in a fight
A-aaaaa
A-wake him up, wake him up, wake
    him up
Call out the C-I-A
A-aaaaa
A-wake him up, wake him up, wake
    him up
Incursion under way
Wake up Ron, wake up Ron, wa-a-a-ke
    up Ron
Wake up Ron, wake up Ron, wa-a-a-ke
    up Ron

Cold War by bridging the humor gap between the two rival superpowers.

"Sure," we said. Viktor then began inquiring about American nuclear proliferation policy, and the lunch began to seem not quite so innocent. Viktor called again a few days later, confirming that high-ranking Soviet authorities very much did want the Capitol Steps to come to Moscow for a "youth festival," to join entertainment troupes from all over the world—Cuba, North Korea, Romania—as long as we agreed to poke fun only at the U.S., not at the Soviet Union. "We don't consider it polite to make fun of our leaders, but it's fine to make fun of yours," Viktor explained.

And so our show-closing song, "We arm the world / We and the Kremlin" would have to be edited to "We arm the world / We," as we marched through Red Square, singing funny songs about Ronald Reagan, right between the North Korean Praise Our Homeland and Curse Capitalist Running Dogs and the North Siberian We Will Bury You Bobsled and Ski-Jumping team.

"Nyet," we told him.

Faced with the choice between going V.I. Lenin or John Lennon, we chose the John route. Capitalism over communism.

Three Kremlin funerals later, while we were singing our "Gorby Gorbachev" song ("Hottest red since Andropov / He's the world's first yuppie slav"), four Soviet generals huffed and puffed, got up, and ceremoniously left the room. They had previously heard us sing our "Hello Dolly" parody about a prominent dissident the Russians had somehow smuggled out of the U.S. ("Hello Vitaly / It's so nice to have you back where you belong"), so we can understand why they were not in a good mood. To paraphrase Viktor, "They didn't consider it polite."

To this day, those Soviet generals remain the only audience members ever to protest our show—except for a crazed Lithuanian, who stood and cheered when he heard us mention his little country, until he realized we were making a joke at its expense, whereupon he stormed out and summoned the manager, who dropped in on us backstage and asked what was going on, whereupon we reminded the hotel manager of the First Amendment.

Lithuania. What a country.

President Reagan's persistent assault on the "Evil Empire" and the budding scourge of terrorist nations delivered one comic topic after another.

We had a cute little war in the Caribbean. ("You say Grenayda / I say Grenahda / He said invada / We used an armada / Grenayda-Grenahda, we used an armada / We blew the whole place up.")

Bombs don't always make for jokes, but they sure did when our Air Force launched a bombing raid from an English airfield, headed for terrorist enclaves in Libya, only to be denied access to French air space. When our pilots got to Libya, they inadvertently bombed the French Embassy. *Quel horreur!* This prompted a song (apologies to "I Could Have Danced All Night") that had our audiences stomping and yelling: "We circled France all night / We had to bank our wings / 'Cuz some Parisian things / Had disapproved our war / We gave a cheer the moment we discovered / A little target in our sight / We only know when we / Blew up their embassy / We could have danced through France all night."

Libyans were believed to be coolly responsible for the murderous explosion of a U.S.-bound passenger plane over Lockerbie, Scotland—not funny—but their antics and alibis afterwards ached for a comic swipe. To the Groucho song "Lydia, the Tattooed Lady," we sang: "Libya O Libya / Have you been to Libya? / Libya the terrorist nation / Just when we are done unpacking / Off we go on some hijacking / Libya O Libya / By air or amphibia / We'll hit the Qaddafi Club Med / At terrorist school, he was known as a dunce / When Abu Nidal had some suicide stunts / He soon volunteered / I'll try anything once / You can learn a lot / If you don't get caught / Aren't you glad you're not in Libya?"

A song about terrorist "suicide stunts"? How could that be amusing? Well, in the 1980s, it was—because the risk still felt so remote to people attending our shows.

When is a joke about human tragedy in good taste, and when not? That's not an easy question, and the best answer is: know your audience. And know the day's news.

★★★★★★★★★★★★★★★★

**Thank God I'm a Contra Boy
(parody of
"Thank God I'm a Country Boy")**

Well, life in Nicaragua's kinda laid back
Livin' in a jungle in a wee little shack
Folks get you, and you try to get 'em back
Thank God I'm a Contra boy
Well, the future's lookin' bleaker and
  bleaker
The Commies' next stop is in Costa Rica
Couple years more, and they'll be in
  Topeka
Yee-hah!
Thank God, I'm a Contra boy, yeah!

For an event in the U.S., even one death can be enough to push a subject off limits, unless the story has such long legs (like the O.J. Simpson trial) that you simply can't ignore it. Foreign adventures pose a more difficult line-drawing exercise. If we had avoided or excised songs for every incident that involved death or human suffering, we would have had nearly no songs about foreign policy.

For example, we've had several songs about Israel, notably our parody of "Cheek to Cheek": "Hebron, I'm in Hebron… / Living Sheik to Sheik." When there's been violence, we rested it for awhile. When there were peace talks, we brought it back. You can tell when it's time, by listening to how audiences respond.

Some tender souls may disagree, but wars invariably produce humor. Maybe that stems from an emotional defense mechanism—you have to either laugh or cry. Wartime jokes are also born of the sheer grandeur of the stage on which great nations play out their roles, and the misadventures that so often result.

Which brings us to Iran-Contra.

In those pre-Internet days, the story broke when a Beirut newspaper, *Al Shirra*, accused the U.S. of having shipped weapons from Israel and the Philippines to Iran, in an effort to win the release of American hostages who had been held in Lebanon. These guns, bullets, and spare parts weren't donated; they were *sold*, with proceeds going to fund the Nicaraguan anti-communist Contra brigades, in apparent violation of a recent act of Congress.

The Iran-Contra scandal had nearly everything. Money, greed, deceit, passion, guns, prisoners, people in funny hats, violence, hypocrites, ridiculous politicians, you name it. Everything, that is, except sex. The closest we got to that was Fawn Hall, coy and comely, but all she ever shredded was documents. But we had the next best thing: accusations of a cover-up.

Here is where the core joke about Reagan worked to his advantage. He didn't know much, because he didn't work hard, and because he slept

★★★

Who Put the Bomb in Tehran Tehran Tehran?
(parody of "Who Put the Bomp in the Bomp She-Bomp She-Bomp?")

REAGAN
I'd like to find the guy who did us wrong
And sent those weapons over to Iran
STAFF
Bow-bow-bow
Who put the bomb in Tehran-Tehran-Tehran?
Who put the bam in Iran for Ayatollah?
Who put the buck in the bank in Switzerland?
Who put the ching in the check the Contras got?
Who wrote that check?
We'd like to break his neck
We'll hang that fellow from the highest tree
Yeah
REAGAN
When my Nancy said
NANCY
Ron, Ronny-Ron, now don't you be a dip-dip
REAGAN
Then I had to find someone to blame
And when I heard her saying

STAFF
Ron Ronny-Ron, now don't you be a ding-dong
REAGAN
I knew a colonel I could name
STAFF
Yeah
OLLIE
Well, I put the bomb, the bomb the bomb-bomb
In Tehran, Tehran, Iran
Yeah, I'm the dip-the dip-tip they indicted, dicted, dicted
Well, if you wanna slama-jama, slama-jama his little
   ding dong
Well, baby, baby, baby, *pardon me*
STAFF
Where did he go?
He ran off with that dough
REAGAN
I'll fire that colonel from the N.S.C.
STAFF
Bomb in Iran go boom
Yeah

a lot. ("A-wake him up, a-wake him up.")

Once our Reagan character woke up, he warned Americans about the Red Menace—how better than through the folksy tune, "Thank God I'm a Country Boy." ("Thank God, I'm a Contra boy, yeah!")

As with all high-profile scandals, a fall-guy had to be found. ("Who put the bomb in Tehran-Tehran-Tehran?")

We found one when we watched Lieutenant Colonel Oliver North spend six mesmerizing days on the witness stand. If it's good TV, it's

THANK GOD I'M A CONTRA BOY 35

★★★★★★★★★★★★★★★★

**We'll Do What Ollie Would
(parody of "Hooray for Hollywood")**

If in Managua, in Nicaragua
Some poor little Contra sitting ducks
Require a mission, with ammunition
But lack winter tires for their trucks
Let's do like we did to help the Shah
Who cares if the plan is not within the law
We'll do what Ollie would
And break the law like Ollie says we could
If Congress dares to pass some crazy
   statute
Who gives a rat's hoot
We'll make a great livelihood
My mother told me I'd make it good
See you in Hollywood

good for humor—and this was the best governmental TV since Watergate. And you have to hand it to Ollie. No less than Madonna or Michael Jackson, he knew how to seize the moment and become more than just another celebrity; he became a *star*.

Our songs about foreign wars and global scandals were always favorite items for overseas visitors who chanced to be in our audience. They often came up to us after shows and told us how, in their home countries, people either whispered or shouted their jokes, whether out of fear or (as in Western Europe) to make and ideological point as brutally as they could.

Over the years, portions of our show have been broadcast overseas as an example of our national sense of humor. Voice of America has played some of our songs to the furthest reaches of the planet. Bill Strauss and Dave Gencarelli once sang our "Immense Expense" song in French ("*Depense immense est surement en defense*") for the benefit of Francophone West Africa, and during another VOA show, one fellow phoned in from China, asking for advice about how to start a political satire troupe. We don't know how Bill's answer translated into Chinese, but he hopes it was some variant of "Very carefully."

Especially during presidential campaigns, we're often visited by camera crews from all over the world, asking us what's so funny about the candidates. Making jokes about the U.S. in front of foreigners can feel a little awkward, as though we're native culturama in indigenous garb, but it's what we do, so we oblige.

We did a show for an audience of Japanese who didn't understand much English, didn't know when to laugh, but applauded wildly after each song, as if to express their respect—and the vain wish that officials in the Japanese Diet could put on a show like this in Tokyo.

"Only in America," our Japanese guests seemed to say, with their silent smiles. Perhaps they were secretly plotting revenge—against which our song warned, "Though we lack engineers, it's true / We have many more lawyers than you / We can sue, we can sue, we can sue, we can sue…"

By the late 1980s, we had become a bustling commercial enterprise. In 1985, Bill Strauss did what every aspiring entertainer is constantly warned not to do: He Quit the Day Job before any real money was coming in, and turned his downstairs den into the Capitol Steps World Headquarters.

Her reputation for humor leading the way, Elaina Newport had found refuge from Percy's defeat by taking an ideal position for a Capitol Stepper: as a legislative staff member for the funniest U.S. senator at the time, Alfonse D'Amato of New York, better known as Senator Pothole. Elaina's supposed job, of course, was to fill potholes, but her *real* job was to write songs and organize casts for shows.

Our cofounder Jim Aidala spent his days at the Congressional Research Service, saving the world from toxic dumps, while spending his nights arranging tech for a cast that was just learning how to use sound and lights, and handle props that no longer were just schlepped around in bags.

Where we'd previously asked the press to stay away, now we desperately wanted them to write loving reviews and long adoring stories about us. Some of them actually did, including the *Wall Street Journal*, which gave us one of those page-one center column only-in-free-market-America articles that, a decade later, would be worth billions to fledgling IPOs.

We were also buoyed by our frequent studio recordings for National Public Radio's *All Things Considered*. Their producers would call us and ask, "Do you have a song on Senator Leahy's new procedural amendments to the bipartisan regulatory reform initiative?" To which we would say, "How amazing you'd ask, because we just wrote a laugh-riot song about exactly that incredibly funny topic." Two hours later, after cobbling together that song, we'd be in the studio recording it, and that night it'd be on the air.

Then came our TV break, thanks to the chairman, guru, and omnipotent leader of Figgie, Incorporated, a company that made everything from baseballs to fire trucks. Harry Figgie first saw us at the Willard Hotel, where he laughed and laughed, liking us so much he soon sponsored a series of Capitol Steps PBS-TV specials. They were quite fun to do, and we would have done more, except Harry Figgie went bankrupt. We hope we had nothing to do with that.

We also began doing quarterly shows for National Public Radio stations, co-produced by KCRW in Santa Monica, California. Since 1988, our "Politics Takes a Holiday" shows have run every New Year's Day, April Fool's Day, Independence Day, and Halloween.

To take advantage of all this media, the lifeblood of any commercial act, we stuffed and licked direct-mail envelopes until our lips chapped. The response was terrific, right from the start, and Bill got to work negotiating contracts with clients who now had to pay for what they used to get for free.

By now, we were entering the doldrums of Reagan's presidency. Old jokes about Ron and Nancy, budget deficits, and Evil Empires no longer had the same kick. The Challenger exploded. No laughs there. Iran-Contra was good, to a point, but we needed more. To push our fees up enough to make a living at this, we needed some funnier things to happen.

For America's burgeoning musical political satire industry, namely ourselves, ever to have a real 1980s greed-is-good experience, we needed a *coup de grace*, one of those classic Norman-Rockwell-boy-meets-girl-boy-loses-pants-girl-meets-press kind of story.

Enter the sorry sailor. Gary Hart, then a U.S. senator from Colorado, a state where they don't sail much. Having risen to fame, sort of, as George McGovern's campaign manager, Hart became a senator known for pursuing arcane subjects. Rumor had it, he actually knew something about a few topics and could speak sensibly about them without staff around, which was fairly unusual in the Senate in those (or any other) days.

He'd already made one run for the Democratic presidential nomination, against Walter Mondale, trying to use the same tactic he'd employed to win McGovern his one state (Massachusetts) against Nixon in '72. He tried to mobilize boomers in some great generational crusade. Not this time. By 1984, boomers were too busy buying minivans, bassinets, and gummy bears to pay attention to Hart's urgent resurrection of the old call to re-take to the streets.

The magnitude of Mondale's loss made Hart the odds-on choice in 1988, a race considered his to lose.

Did he ever. But in doing so, Gary Hart delivered a very large gift to the American comedy industry. Always quick to deny rumors about

 **SIXTEEN SCANDALS**

his extracurricular estrogenic fascinations, he'd dared reporters to follow him and see what kind of life he actually led. A couple of enterprising reporters actually took him up on his challenge, and came away with photos of a smiley leggy blonde named Donna Rice sitting on Gary-the-sailor's lap on the *Monkey Business*, somewhere on the sea lanes to the Bahamas. Next came little him-and-her photos taken from the bushes of a Capitol Hill townhouse where Donna stayed a tad late a night or two.

The austere 1980s had at long last erupted in a good old-fashioned steamy and slimy snake-and-apple story, one far sexier than anything the old Wayne Hayses, Wilbur Millses, or later-model Ted Kennedys could muster. He was OK looking, she was gorgeous, and—quite unlike other erotic scandals of our time—they appeared to be romancing the *GQ* meets *Cosmo* girl way. With money. On yachts. In beds (with, one presumes, very fluffy mattresses).

Crowds flocked to our shows, to see what we were doing on Gary and Donna.

Quite unlike the scandals in the decade to come, this *Monkey Business* story—and our various songs and skits about these two love birds—didn't last very long. Neither did Hart's presidential run. In a matter of weeks, he had quit Washington, returned to seclusion, and asked the world to leave him be.

We did, in due course. In comedy, you usually find audiences shifting their attitudes from glee to sympathy—and losing their propensity to laugh—within weeks, even days, after your target leaves the public eye. What had happened with Walter Mondale, a succession of dead Soviet premiers, and Oliver North was echoed by Gary Hart.

The void was preciously brief, filled by televangelists Jim and Tammy Faye Bakker and their PTL (Praise The Lord, alias Pass The Loot), and sex lioness Jessica Hahn. The comedy ran thicker than Tammy's makeup, and quicker than her tears. We rocked, jokes rolled, and audiences roared.

Month by glorious month, the satirical landscape was broadening and deepening. Humor spigoted out like never before in our country's history, or so it sure felt at the time. Sure, Wall Street crashed in October 1987, but in our industry, biz was booming.

Around that time, fueled by this new prosperity, we went through a bit of a corporate transmogrification, from a 501(c)(3) nonprofit "charity" to a real for-profit humor Virginia corporation. In 1987, we moved from a cast that wanted the Steps to remain a part-time hobby to a cast prepared to make a full professional commitment, including Anne Hill, Ann Schmitt, Brian Ash, and Mike Loomis, who have been with us ever since.

We settled into a funky new nightclub, Chelsea's, in the heart of Georgetown, and secured a lease on a townhouse in Alexandria's toney Old Town. Elaina quit her Senate job and became full-time producer. After three years in the basement of Bill's house, the Capitol Steps had entered the big time.

Even so, we were concerned about the future. We'd built our rapidly expanding political satire business through the eight-year presidency of Ronald Reagan, and we couldn't imagine that the next president would be nearly as funny.

We needn't have worried.

5

Bush Lite
("Read My Flips")

★★★★★★★★★
TRACKS: 13–15

Occasionally, in the Capitol Steps history, we've been accused of causing the scandals that provide us with material. And no matter how many times we've denied having told Monica to save that dress, or Nancy Reagan to consult an astrologer, we are sometimes suspiciously ahead of the curve.

For example, in the spring of 1989, with trouble brewing in Panama, we imagined a fictitious scenario in a parody of the song "We Need a Little Christmas," which became something about needing "a little isthmus."

We sang this in the spring and summer of 1989. In early autumn, we recorded it on our *Danny's First Noël* Christmas album.

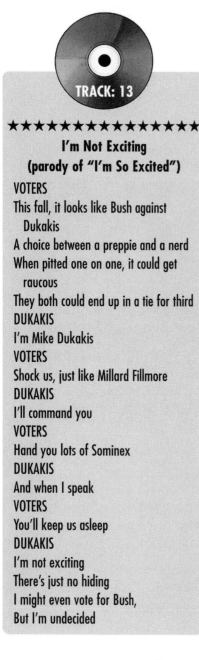

TRACK: 13

★★★★★★★★★★★★★★★★

**I'm Not Exciting
(parody of "I'm So Excited")**

VOTERS
This fall, it looks like Bush against
  Dukakis
A choice between a preppie and a nerd
When pitted one on one, it could get
  raucous
They both could end up in a tie for third
DUKAKIS
I'm Mike Dukakis
VOTERS
Shock us, just like Millard Fillmore
DUKAKIS
I'll command you
VOTERS
Hand you lots of Sominex
DUKAKIS
And when I speak
VOTERS
You'll keep us asleep
DUKAKIS
I'm not exciting
There's just no hiding
I might even vote for Bush,
But I'm undecided

In the fall, some D.C. radio stations played it—and, no doubt, some Pentagon brass heard it. In December, the U.S. invaded Panama. Our song was actually prophetic, right down to giving Manuel (Noriega) the business and being home by Christmas.

Panama wasn't the largest military adventure in U.S. history, but it might well have been the funniest—one of those "rip and read" events comedians love so much, where the jokes just drip off the news. Like how they supposedly played "Panama" by Van Halen at maximum volume outside, to torture the poor dictator. Or how Noriega had a face like a pineapple, a villain straight from central casting. Banana Republicans? ("Yes, We Have No Bananas" became "Yes, we have No-Riega. We have No-Riega today.")

The hunt for Noriega yielded us a classic moment in our history—the one time we successfully parodied a favorite song ("The Vatican Rag") by the favorite political satirist of our childhood, Tom Lehrer. ("If you are an ex-dictator / North or south of the equator / If you face a downfall / Give a call to John Paul / Under the Vatican Flag.")

Through it all, George Herbert Walker Bush sat tall in the saddle, with his crooked grin, showing off what he'd learned as the youngest combat fighter in the Navy (legend had it) in World War II. He proved to be a tad better with troop movements than historical dates, though. In one of those momentary lapses politicians hate but comics adore, he declared September 7 as Pearl Harbor Day—giving us "fantastick" fodder with "Try to Remember / That Date in September / The day Japan attacked Pearl Harbor," a song the president himself thrice sang onstage with us. (We use the term "sang" loosely.) Each time, the audience went nuts.

Where the Reagan years brought a resurgence of American political comedy, the Bush I years kicked it into a new gear. And where Reagan was an actor, George Bush was America's sitcom dad. To our boomer cast members, it was as if we'd graduated from *Shaggy Dog* movies and reached an adulthood in which Fred MacMurray actually was U.S. president, as though the 1960s and '70s had never happened. A new world order? Yeah, dad, sure, dad, whatever you say, dad. To the Gen Xers in our troupe, like Mark Eaton, "He seemed more like a grandfather than an elected official. Something about him was very comforting and 'normal.'"

Back in the early 1980s, in "Get Me to the Dirge on Time," we had introduced George Bush to our audiences as Reagan's amiable, rather inconsequential sidekick, whose most frequent assignment was attending state funerals back when Soviet premiers were dying in rapid succession ("Who's getting buried in the morning?"). Dave Gencarelli played Bush with an airy, gangly nonchalance, bristling with goshes and golly gees, all WASPy and preppy, paper and plastic with nary a hint of steel—the kind of guy who would sing "nyah, nyah, nyah-nyah nyah" to a foreign dictator in the closing chorus of our parody of "The Night They Drove Old Dixie Down."

Bush had actually run against Reagan in 1980 (remember that?) and apparently made a stronger impression on the Gipper than on the rest of the country. If the national memory of the elder Bush as vice president is vague, so is the indisputable fact that any American under age forty-five has never voted in an election that didn't have a Bush or a Dole on the ticket, and the other somewhere around.

So, comedically, one can look back at the early and middle 1980s and see a few scratchings on the trees of time—George was here: hi there, it's me—but to the national memory bank, he was like the corporate guy who came to work on time, poured coffee at the meetings, helped collate and staple the annual reports, and then got The Big Promotion.

That, of course, was in 1988. Never, in the years between 1984 and 1992, did America ever see such an undistinguished field of candidates, which we celebrated in our song (and album), "76 Unknowns." Who were the Democrats in that year's huge field? You don't want to know. Suffice to say, Michael Dukakis beat them all.

When Michael D spoke, America listened. To another channel.

★★★★★★★★★★★★★★★★★

Fifty Ways to Hide New Taxes
(parody of
"Fifty Ways to Leave Your Lover")

BUSH
You heard my campaign promise that I'd
    never raise your tax
And if I try, I know that I would face
    right-wing attacks
But since I got myself elected, well, I've
    seen the budget facts
Now I've got fifty ways to hide new taxes
Nifty ways to hide new taxes
Just call it a fee, Lee
A revenue plan, Stan
Just cough up the dough, Moe
It's an S&L fee
DEMOCRAT
You're so outta luck schmuck
We just heard quacking from this duck...
The moment it quacks, Max
We'll know it's a tax

At the Democratic convention in 1988, the halls were not red, white, and blue (too old school), but mauve, taupe, and gray. To complete that scheme, they didn't need to bring anything gray. They already had Dukakis.

In our parody "I'm Not Exciting" to "I'm So Excited," the best argument Dukakis could give for voting for him was "I'm Not Indicted." His personality was so infectious, we invented a disease, "Electducoccus," afflicting anyone who actually voted for him.

As the campaign wore on, "The Duke" made the blunder of attempting to remind everyone he was a veteran by climbing aboard a tank with a helmet on, looking like a half-asleep Woody Allen in a *M.A.S.H.* episode. This prompted our song "Tanks for the Memories," where we depicted him as a snoozy manboy with a helmet and a toy tank.

The electoral result? One of the *Naked Gun* movies showed three photos on a wall of disasters: The *Hindenberg*, the *Titanic*, and the Dukakis.

Almost from the instant Bush won, *Saturday Night Live's* Dana Carvey set the classic caricature with his John-Wayne-meets-Mr.-Rogers George Bush Sr. impersonation. By the end of Bush's term, no comedian could play Bush without doing a parody of Dana Carvey's parody. Audiences expected that. Playing the post-Inaugural George Bush, our Dave Werner added a tilted walk that reminded people of a praying mantis running into the sunlight, a study in lines and angles in perpetual motion. Add carefully paralleled arm swoops, long-fingered hands playing shadow puppets, and you get the picture: America's Geek-in-Chief. The boomers who dominated our audience liked Bush to be portrayed this way, because if the U.S. president was this geeky, that made everybody else feel way hip.

Bush had a way of chewing on words, doubling them, tripling them, recasting some anonymous speechwriter's careful craftsmanship into what you might see in a cartoon cloud. If we felt a little talked down to, it all seemed quaintly fatherly, albeit a tad out of joint for a man in a blue power suit. Golf plaids—now that might have fit the style better.

Like him or not, George projected a harmless/clueless image of the kind of guy you'd love to have as a father-in-law.

Part of what made George Bush so funny, for people a little over half his age, was that the age-old generation gap had come down to *this*. Here was this guy who had cut his political teeth back in the days of Richard Nixon—some oddly aged mixture of an elite-establishment, Ivy League, button-down Rockefeller Republican and a baked-plains, oil-wildcatting, Houston-Lubbock shirt-tanned Goldwaterite. This guy was *president?*

Our parents' generation's first and last U.S. presidents had come from Hyannisport and Kennebunkport, two coyly cute New England beach resort towns, but that's where the similarity ended.

John Kennedy—stylish, artsy, and handsome—played touch football on the beach. George Bush zoomed around the quiet Maine waters in a cigarette boat. Where John Kennedy seemed to have been groomed for the presidency, like a new American royalty, George Bush was a from-everywhere-and-nowhere guy who, at the tail end of the Vietnam War, tried to get himself elected to the Senate from Texas, but failed. Twenty years earlier, our college classmates would have thrown pigs' blood at such a person. Now they contributed to his campaign. Pretty funny.

All right, so we knew from the outset that George would never make it to Mt. Rushmore—mainly because his wife Barbara was already there, masquerading as George Washington (or was it the other way around?). She immediately endeared herself to the nation's women with her sly motherly repartee. "Somewhere out in this audience may even be someone who will one day follow in my footsteps and preside over the White House as the president's spouse," she told a Wellesley commencement gathering. "I wish him well." Such an attitude made her immensely popular among young women, who so wanted to "be like Bar." "Remember," she warned them at Wellesley, "they only name things after you when you're dead or really old."

TRACK: 15

★★★★★★★★★★★★★★★★★

**We Need a Little Isthmus
(parody of
"We Need a Little Christmas")**

GENERAL
Call out the Army
You need a brand new war to lift your
spirits up
BUSH
That won't alarm me
But do you think I should send troops to
Panama now
GENERAL
George, you need a little isthmus
Right this very minute
Give Manuel the business
If you now begin it
We could all be home by Christmas
We might even win it
Need a little isthmus now

How to portray her in our show? Where we'd dressed Nancy Reagan in red, we put Bar in blue, with a pearl necklace. We were tempted to take a cue from the *Saturday Night Live* cast, and have a guy play her (like Phil Hartman in pearls), but we staved off rebellion from our female cast by fitting them for white wigs.

Always a good sport with an easy laugh, Barbara was motherly, protective, always sweet, yet totally frank with us. She saw us perform a half-dozen times, and we remember more than one occasion when she parsed our lyrics afterwards, letting us know if we got beyond PG-13. At one Christmas show we did for the Bushes, their family, and the White House staff, we sang a slightly edgy song about Madonna, Santa Claus, some reindeer, and inter-mammal relationships, after which Barbara got her index finger wagging about whether that was a Capitol Steps sort of thing to do.

In those days, George was riding an approval rating of over 80 percent. But on the heels of a popular war came a most unpopular recession and George's famous tactical blunder. We wish we'd been a fly on the wall when George had negotiated that line with his speechwriters back at the 1988 GOP convention. *Invigilate my mandible.* Cold. *Reconnoiter my larynx.* Warmer. *Lookee my pie-hole.* Real warm. *Read my lips.* Hot.

"Read my lips. No new taxes," was a simple sound bite for a simple sound-bite culture. ("Why ask why." "Just do it." "No excuses.") But it caused George to step right into Texas pancake. Whether downmarket or upmarket, "no" meant no, "new" meant new, and "taxes" meant—well, that was open to some interpretation, as we helped George try to explain, to the tune of "Fifty Ways to Raise Your Taxes" ("Just call it a fee, Lee").

Supply siders were demanding his scalp. Meanwhile, White House Chief of Staff John "Air" Sununu kept the nation laughing with his travels on military planes. ("Glory, glory, how Sununu / Got himself in deepest doo-doo / With the places that he flew to.")

A price was paid, in more than mere comedy. In 1992, ol' George went out the way he came in, as everybody's favorite clueless dad. Some reporter asked him what a bar code was, and he honestly didn't know. Maybe he thought it was some secret formula by which first lady Bar kept the secrets of real life (like how to buy a half-gallon of milk) beyond his reach.

But he tried to be everybody's president. The Education President. The Environment President. The I'm a Good Guy and Isn't America Neat President. He was less a leader than the emcee of "a thousand points of light in a broad and peaceful sky."

Bush Lite. Tastes great. Not too filling.

What we all wanted, but couldn't find was "oh, the vision thing," as he himself once put it. We leaned close to our TV sets trying to find meaning and wisdom in the words his speechwriters had stuffed in his mouth. "And now, we can see a new world coming into view," he once said. "A world in which there is the very real prospect of a new world order." Wow. Most people were doing OK—the Capitol Steps certainly were—so we didn't mind that words like that meant absolutely nothing.

The subtext was all that mattered. Comfort, homeyness, a mannerly decorum—all producing a comedy that, in hindsight, may have been more dismissive than biting. We could expect a guy like George to run a war or manage an economy (maybe), but no way would any boomer in his or her right mind ever ask this man to choose the tapes for a car trip, or choose from a menu, or even pick a necktie.

Sure, he would lose the 1992 election to someone way funnier, but our troupe had a real fine time with (as he now calls himself) "the old guy." He invited us to perform several times at events he hosted, and was always eager to jump on stage to the delight of everyone present. He had a wonderful capacity for allowing himself to get down and

★★★★★★★★★★★★★★★★

16 Funniest Political Oxymorons

1. Holy war
2. Airport security
3. Mrs. Clinton
4. Compassionate conservative
5. Liberal values
6. Campaign reform
7. Postal Service
8. Democratic leadership
9. Justice Scalia
10. Legal principles
11. Political promise
12. Senatorial courtesy
13. Congressional ethics
14. Legislative restraint
15. Media scrutiny
16. Military intelligence

silly, out of the public eye. It's one of the reasons why, of all the U.S. presidents of our lifetime, he is known to be the one most beloved by his staff—and, we suspect, by other performers at White House events.

As George himself once proclaimed, at the start of his successful bid for the presidency, "What's wrong with being a boring kind of guy?"

Read our quips: America had fun on your watch, George Herbert Walker Bush—not boring at all.

SIXTEEN SCANDALS

6

Stand by Your Dan
("I Want a Man with a Slow Mind")

★★★★★★★★

TRACKS: 16–18

"Who do you think I should pick as vice president?" the elder George Bush asked of us at a show in the spring of 1988.

"Pick someone funny," Elaina Newport replied.

The rest is history.

We can't claim that George Bush Sr. spent massive amounts of time consulting with the Capitol Steps (no, we weren't responsible for his famous tax increase), but that particular incident occurred on the heels of a dinner for Australian President Robert Hawke at the vice president's residence. We had arrived to find the Bush family engrossed in a game of horseshoes. Photos taken at the time depict members of the Capitol Steps tossing

★★★★★★★★★★★★★★★★

**Stand by Your Dan
(parody of "Stand by Your Man")**
BUSH
Stand by your Dan
Though fellas think he's sappy
He'll make girl voters happy
And that's my plan
I think we can
Get Bush and Quayle elected
That's why I will not dump this man
Stand by your Dan

horseshoes dangerously close to the head of the Leader of the Free World.

We joined the state dinner, then did a little show at which we sang a song about Australia, along with some bits about the Reagans, the Democrats, the presidential primaries—the usual. Here we were, not long after Super Tuesday and the New York primary cinched the top spot for Mr. Bush, still more than two months before the Republican convention, with the future president asking us about his choice of running mate.

So while we now feel, in hindsight, responsible for Dan Quayle being selected as vice president, at the time that he was picked, it was not immediately obvious how funny he would be—nor the role comedians would soon play in our postmodern system of government, as a new "check and balance" on political king-making. Where Reagan had added one new qualifier for circa-1980s leadership (the capacity to "laugh with" a joke at one's own expense), Quayle added a new one (not to be "laughed at").

From Quayle forward, the "laugh at" factor became a new anxiety for candidates and a serious headache for their image makers. It's not great to spend ten million dollars crafting an image of statesmanship on highly produced ads in expensive major markets, when the late-night comics get audiences to howl just by quoting you verbatim.

Why did Quayle trip this "laugh at" cord? Four reasons. His looks, his background (and generation), his foot-in-mouth disease, and his emergence as conservative Culture Warrior. Add to this the realization that, wow, this guy truly could become president. Tangle it all in the emerging Culture War between left and right, and you got a laugh trap from which the man simply couldn't exit.

At first impression, in the summer of 1988, he seemed to all the world to have been chosen pretty much exclusively for his looks—in his case, of the blonde Ken doll variety. Pretty face candidacies aren't new in American history, as the rise of Warren Harding and John Kennedy would attest. The cutest candidate of the nineteenth century (Franklin Pierce) even got elected before women could vote, and despite a lackluster pre–Civil War presidency, he succeeded in getting a college named after him. (Dan Quayle College? Now there's a thought.)

Yet Dan was the first candidate to ply the cutesy factor in the post-feminist era. Not good timing. It was as though Bush, in applying the "vision thing," felt that this was what women of the 1980s craved in a leader. It definitely struck a nerve—with the nation and our audiences—albeit not the one Bush intended.

In our first response, we featured a female performer, Amy Felices Young, idolizing an actual blonde Ken doll. Everyone knows that when you undress a Ken doll, there's nothing there. In Quayle's case, that suggested that there wasn't much *V* to go along with the not-much *P* in the aspiring VP. In another sketch, we tweaked Dan's TV-game-show-looks by implying that George Bush had actually meant to select *Wheel of Fortune's* Pat Sajak, but goofed and picked his identical twin instead. In our "Stand by Your Dan" song, we painted a picture of Quayle being selected mainly because, well, someone needs to mow the White House lawn. Other comics were making similar points. *Saturday Night Live* borrowed a real-live little kid to play the man who would be a heartbeat away from the president.

The real Dan dressed like a junior Rotarian (not much humor there). To depict him in our show, we chose a melange of three images—clueless, childlike, and Mork-ish—a blondie in a helicopter beanie, with rainbow suspenders. Performers who played Dan gave him a shuffly, rhythmless walk, and the kind of flat fingery wave a five-year-old gives you on his birthday. You didn't even need to say, "Hi, I'm Danny Quayle." The audience knew exactly whom we meant. Later, we added "I Was Elected Vice President, and All I Got Was This Lousy T-Shirt."

The Quayle voice depended on the performer. Those who were more sympathetic to the man went for juvenility. Those who were not went for imbecility. "With Dan Quayle you have to decide whether to play him as a child or as an idiot," said Brian Ash. "I finally settled on both."

Beyond how Quayle looked lay the second factor, of what he in fact was. He and Bush. They represented separate and very unalike generations. Dan was a boomer, exactly one day older than Bill Strauss. When Lloyd Bentsen craftily said to him, "You are no Jack Kennedy," that was more than just a personal insult.

For the first time, merely being a boomer hit that "laugh at" button. And, for the first time, we had a colossal comedic target from our own generation. Back then, nobody had yet discovered Generation X, and boomers—then pushing forty—still thought of themselves as America's campus kids. Now we had (gasp) someone roughly our age who was vice president. Back in those heady days of campus riots, running the country (and not just protesting against those who did) was the last thing on our minds. As Dan himself declared, when named, "I did not know in 1969 that I would be in this room today."

Dan wasn't as hip as most boomers then considered themselves, but he did have one crucial generational badge: by all accounts, he had been a semi-sort-of draft dodger, back in the days of Vietnam. So had most of his peers, which lent Dan's dilemma a certain "everyman" quality. But, unlike his peers, Dan wasn't willing to shrug it off as a '60s sort of thing, but instead tried to appear to all the world as an ultra-earnest good boy, utterly oblivious to the humor maelstrom. In his eyes, his draft record didn't disqualify him from being the leader of the free world, with a finger on the nuclear trigger. As Dan himself put it, "I don't have to experience tragedy to understand it." (Sure, but what about comedy?) Had he either fought in the war or marched to stop it, he might have connected with his peers a little better.

Thus did it become true that, long before Bill Clinton stood accused of being a far more aggressive draft dodger, Dan Quayle was pounded in the press for his National Guard Service. That was more uniformed service than performed by most of his male peers (and nearly all his female peers) in that riotous college class of 1969. To his peers, if not to Dan, the real story was that Quayle had a father (and a publisher father-in-law) capable of pulling strings in a small-town Indiana elite sort of way. As Dan himself said in 1988: "I do...I do...I do what any normal person would do at that age. You call home. You call home to mother and father and say, 'I'd like to get into the National Guard.'"

The problem was, Dan carried on about it like some not-well-remembered dormmate-from-hell, the guy who kept trying to redefine his good luck (for having been well-born) into some high moral calling. A lot of boomers had known guys like that, so Dan's own good fortune (getting into the National Guard, while ten thousand others languished

SIXTEEN SCANDALS

★★

16 Funniest Non-Scandal Quotes

1. "P-O-T-A-T-O-E" (Dan Quayle)
2. "Read my lips. No new taxes." (George Bush Sr.)
3. "You teach a child to read, and he or her will be able to pass a literacy test." (George W. Bush)
4. "I have said that I'm not running and I'm having a great time being pres—... being a first-term senator." (Hillary Clinton)
5. "For seven and a half years I've worked alongside President Reagan. We've had triumphs. Made some mistakes. We've had some sex...uh...setbacks." (George Bush Sr.)
6. "I was recently on a tour of Latin America, and the only regret I have was that I didn't study Latin harder in school so I could converse with those people." (Dan Quayle)
7. "Now, like, I'm president. It would be pretty hard for some drug guy to come into the White House and start offering it up, you know?...I bet if they did, I hope I would say, 'Hey, get lost. We don't want any of that.'" (George Bush Sr.)
8. "A mere forty years ago, beach volleyball was just beginning. No bureaucrat would have invented it, and that's what freedom is all about." (Newt Gingrich)
9. "These terrorist acts and, you know, the responses have got to end in order for us to get the framework, the groundwork, not framework, the groundwork, to discuss a framework for peace, to lay the,... all right." (George W. Bush)
10. "They misunderestimated me." (George W. Bush, on the 2000 election)
11. "On the first date, I went, 'Hmmm, he'll be president.'" (Tipper Gore)
12. "This race is tight like a too-small bathing suit on a too-long ride home from the beach." (Dan Rather, on the 2000 election)
13. "I only have on one layer of makeup. I'm incognito." (Katherine Harris)
14. "Where else in the world could you stand on a corner and have people yell 'Go home!' in every language?" (Hillary Clinton, describing New York City)
15. "I am not worried about the deficit. It is big enough to take care of itself." (Ronald Reagan)
16. "I may not have been the greatest president, but I've had the most fun eight years." (Bill Clinton)

on the waiting list) hit close to home in a negative way. Dan was caught cold in the act of having been part of the Me Generation. He could plead not guilty all he wanted, but when the comedic court tried the case, the jury of the audience convicted.

Satire is equal parts truth, exaggeration, and nonsense—the last of which came into play as we got laughs at the expense not of what Dan had done, but what he'd do next. If the Quayle daddy was able to get

TRACK: 17

★★★★★★★★★★★★★★★★★

I Want a Man with a Slow Mind
(parody of
"I Want a Man with a Slow Hand")

MARILYN

When Marilyn Quayle went and married
   a male
I chose a man who never thinks twice
He is my ingenue, 'cuz his tiny IQ
Makes this fellow so perfect for vice
With a look that excites, like a deer in
   the lights
His eyes are so open and dull
And when the moon's bright, he can
   take all night
To screw in a bulb
I want a man with a
Slow mind
My sweet potato doesn't
Spell so good, oooh
He spent his evenin's watchin' *Murphy
   Brown*
Instead of *Mister Rogers Neighborhood*
Will Danny ever win the Presidency?
I think the answer could be
N-O
E!

his C-plus student into the coveted National Guard, maybe he'd also managed to get the vice presidential nod for his son, and if he could do that…oh my. This thin-resuméed boomer boy could rise and rise and rise to, well…anything. We had a song in which Dan's dad revealed his intent to declare the boy pope (Dan the First).

Later, it was reported that he had gotten into law school through an experimental Indiana University program intended to offer "equal opportunity" to minorities, the economically disadvantaged, and students of different viewpoints and backgrounds, and then the real comedic paydirt of the Bush-Quayle Administration emerged: Dan as a shallow pond, the stunted tree in the oak forest, a dented Toyota in a showroom of new BMWs.

The entire world was in on this joke, and the real Dan had the unfortunate tendency of stoking it constantly—like when, for a planned trip to Beijing, he feared for turmoil, until his security advisor reportedly informed him that it was safe, given that "They are only harassing intellectuals." Yikes. When comments like that got reported, fortyish boomers rolled their eyes, thinking "Is this the best we can do?" (To which a twenty-five-year-old in the as-yet-unnamed Gen X would answer: Yes.)

Thus do we reach the third factor in making Dan Quayle such a laugh target. He simply could not speak in public without misspeaking: "If we do not succeed, we run the risk of failure." "The importance of bondage between parent and child." "What a waste it is to lose one's mind. Or not to have a mind is being very wasteful."

Quaylespeak soon became the basis for our most enduring song about the man: "Talk Like a Dan," in which Quayle, played by Dave Gencarelli with vapid confidence, announced his intention to spearhead NASA's efforts to "land a man on the sun," then, realizing it would be awfully hot, added that they would "land him at night."

These comments prompted a "President's Prayer Club," with even the most liberal partisan rooting for George Bush's good health. This became a theme of perhaps the biggest hit of the early Quayle years, our song entitled "Keep Him Alive," which dealt with the unthinkable. Should anything happen to George Bush, Dan Quayle would have his finger on the button. Our song featured a team of doctors, agonizing over the president's every hangnail.

In time, thanks to a spelling error, Quayle jokes metastasized to the point where they became a huge political problem for the beleaguered veep. One day, Dan dropped in on a spelling bee at a Trenton, New Jersey, elementary school. "P-O-T-A-T-O," a student wrote on the blackboard. To which Dan said: "Add one little bit on the end…Think of 'potatoe,' how's it spelled? You're right phonetically, but what else?" When the boy dutifully added an "e," Dan said, "There ya go…all right!"

Years later, the nation's comic emporia were still echoing with laughter over that one. Were we being fair? In this case, yes. Now, we know a lot of political people, some of whom (believe it or not) are actually our friends. Like the rest of us, they get tired, or distracted, or annoyed, or maybe just make some little goofball mistake now and then. But unlike us, they have to maneuver through a world in which every one of their utterances is either on camera or phoned in to a reporter or gossip columnist somewhere.

Many politicians, we're sure, are terrible spellers, or couldn't add a column of figures, even if they are very good at remembering names, raising campaign cash, making opposing positions sound identical, and other essential tools of modern statescraft. But nearly all national leaders have a skill Dan didn't have: the ability to change the subject. When it came to spelling, Dan just couldn't do that.

Why? His "potatoe" gaffe spoke to a real national anxiety about his fitness—and, even worse for him, that wasn't his only spelling goof. The Quayles' 1989 Christmas card read "May our nation continue to be the beakon [sic] of hope to the world." And some letterhead found in Quayle's White House office by incoming Clinton staffers read "Office of the Vice President…the Council on Competativeness." This opened all sorts of comic possibilities. If Dan became president, would NATO become NATOE?

By throwing spuds, Dan's enemies could mash him into hash. Some clown dumped a truckload of potatoes by his house. When Quayle threatened to hold up a copy of Al Gore's book *Earth in the Balance* during the 1992 vice presidential debates, the Gore staff threatened to have their man hold up a potato if he did—so Quayle dropped the idea like a hot, well…potatoe.

The final funny Quayle laugh factor—Dan as Culture Warrior—erupted when, addressing the Commonwealth Club of San Francisco, he criticized Candice Bergen in her role as Murphy Brown. According to Quayle, the sitcom star's having a child out of wedlock was an example of the cultural decay caused by Hollywood. Later, Dan admitted he had never watched the show. The next day, we were parodying "Bad, Bad, Murphy Brown," prompting the other Dan (Rather)'s network to send a camera crew to broadcast our gibe nationwide.

There's nothing wrong, and often something very right, about a national leader taking on Hollywood. But when you do, expect the La-La-Land defense to include some of their famous weapons: star power, entertainment shows, and (especially) late-night comics. Leno and Letterman hooted so loudly over Quayle's Murphy Brown "gaffe" that, months later, when the esteemed *Atlantic Monthly* conceded on its cover that, yes, he'd made a sound point about unwed motherhood, the vice president still came out second-best in the comic tug-of-war. Everywhere except around the coffee bar of the Heritage Foundation and other conservative think-tanks, the jokes still came at the expense of Dan Quayle, not Candice Bergen.

Unfortunately for his wife Marilyn, a fellow as funny as Dan brings everyone around him into his own personal comedy network. By all accounts, Marilyn Quayle wasn't such a funny person, but thanks to Dan, she became so. No one knew quite what Marilyn saw in Dan (although Dan himself was quoted as saying, "She was attracted to me by my intellectual curiosity," in November 1992), so we attempted to explain it in a takeoff of the Pointer Sisters' song "Slow Hand," which became Marilyn singing "I Want a Man with a Slow Mind." The idea was that Marilyn was actually turned on by those deer-in-the-head-lights-eyes, and the way he put the "vice" in vice president. Anne Willis Hill sang this in a Marilyn Quayle pageboy wig, sticking her teeth out as far as possible. (Sorry, Marilyn, but it came with the territory.)

One time, when we performed in the East Room of the White House, Dan and Marilyn were there. We'd gone a little easy on the two of them there, but the vice president came up to us and said he'd heard our stuff about him and thought it was all pretty funny. He was quite nice about it. Later, as the crowd milled in the foyer, Bill Strauss saw Dan standing all alone, drink in hand, as though he were lost and didn't know anybody there. Bill walked over to him and chatted for a while, thinking it'd take maybe ten or twelve seconds before a lobbyist came up to tug on his sleeve and pitch a strip-mine somewhere—that's what usually happens when you talk with a president, vice president, or senator—but absolutely no one seemed to want to talk with the vice president of the United States after our show was over. So he and Bill did the small talk about families, jobs, lives, for several minutes until Bill ran out of things to say (which doesn't happen much).

For a while, we could have written a whole show about Dan Quayle. Every blonde joke you've ever heard fit him perfectly, as when he arrived on stage, breathless, announcing that he was sorry for being late, but (quoting our Dan, not the real one) "there was a power outage and I've been stuck for hours on the escalator."

In time, many of these jokes grew to the point where they still live on in Internet lore. Do a Web search on "Quayle quotes," and before you hit the "print" button, make sure your printer has lots of paper. What you'll see is over the top and in some ways unfair, but if life is unfair, comedy is even less so. We're sure Dan would be the first to laugh it off and tell you: if you can't take the needling, now and forever, don't go into politics.

When Quayle burst into comedy in the 1988 campaign season, he was not the only funny candidate (President Dukakis? Please), which

TRACK: 18

★★★★★★★★★★★★★★★★

**Keep Him Alive
(parody of "Stayin' Alive")**

QUAYLE
Well, just as sure as my name is
   Danny Quayle
I get George's job, should his heart fail
At first, his temperature was fine
Then the nurses screamed
It's ninety-nine!
But he's all right, he's okay
Doctor says he's on the way
Is our George turnin' blue?
Don't let Georgie catch the flu
Things look really dire
He's gonna get a virus, gotta
Keep him alive, keep him alive
When we hear him sniffle
All the nation's in a tiffle
Will the doctor arrive, doctor arrive
BUSH
Ah ah ah ah
QUAYLE
Georgie survive
BUSH
Ah choo

gave us a nice two-fer. That fall, we sold two mix-and-match bumper stickers "Bush-Bentsen: The Texas Twins" and "Dukakis-Quayle: The Duke and the Fluke." Which of those two bumper stickers outsold the other, by four to one? Humor trumps competence, any day.

Four years later, we sweated out the possibility that George Bush would choose a new running mate in 1992. Larry King asked Quayle about this in July 1992, and he assured King that "if I thought I was hurting the ticket, I'd be gone." Quayle went on to assure the public that "the president is going to lead us out of this recovery. It will happen," at a campaign stop at the University of Fresno in 1992, proving that a second term would be as comedically fruitful as the first.

Did Dan Quayle hurt George Bush in 1992? Did Quayle deliver the election to Bill Clinton and Al Gore, thereby giving the greatest gift of all (yes, even greater than Dan!) to comedians for years to come? Perhaps Our Man Dan felt that, having done all he could, it was time to passe the torche.

Later, Dan would briefly flirt with the idea of running for president on his own. Each time any word of a Quayle Exploratory Committee popped out, comedians (including us) put him back in our shows. In a sense, standing jokes about a defeated candidate can act like antibodies against an old virus, providing the nation with a ready-to-go defense against an unwanted recurrence. The political fundraisers would hear the jokes, look at their wallets, and shake their heads sideways. No surprise, then, that Dan couldn't get his own candidacy going.

Herein lies the service political satirists perform, in the national interest. Just like the military, by its presence, wards off foreign invasion—or the courts and police, by their presence, ward off crime—we, by our presence, ward off candidates who seem to be too funny to attain high office. Since Dan, we've had two totally well-behaved, incredibly intelligent presidents. (So much for that theory.)

Even so, we're grateful to Dan Quayle. Truly. Thanks largely to him, the Bush I years marked the fastest growth spurt in Capitol Steps history, and many other comedians also prospered. The way we looked at it was this: a president tries to appease different constituencies through different Cabinet selections. The EPA Administrator may be chosen to please environmentalists, Secretary of Agriculture to deal with farmers, and so forth. Dan Quayle was this president's way of taking care of the comedians, nothing more, nothing less.

That's all right. The American people will take a good laugh over a good cry any day.

7

Operation Stormin' Norman
("Bomb Bomb Iraq")

★★★★★★★★
TRACKS: 19–21

"K-K-Kuwaitis, let's help the Kuwaitis."
The date: Tuesday, January 15, 1991.
"Let's attack-ack-ack-ack Iraq-aq-aq if we can."
The place: Cal Tech, in Pasadena, California.
"Bomb bomb bomb, bomb bomb Iraq."
The time: 8:00 P.M. (PST)
"Bomb bomb bomb, bomb bomb Iraq."
It was exactly one hour before the deadline set by President Bush for Saddam Hussein to begin withdrawing Iraqi troops from Kuwait.

"Let's bomb Ira-a-aq."

TRACK: 19

★★★★★★★★★★★★★★★

Iraq Is Robbin'
(parody of "Rockin' Robin")

Iraq is in the desert all the day long
Arabs and camels are singin' this song
Haughty little Saudi, sneaky oil Sheik
Little Saudi army is weak, weak, weak
Iraq is robbin', *ha ha*
Sheik, sheik sheik
Iraq is robbin', *ha ha*
Sheik, sheedily-sheik
Iraq is robbin'
And the gulf is gonna rock tonight

We were beginning a two-hour show. At intermission, everyone would know whether the U.S. did in fact have a little war on its hand.

"Yeah, let's atta-a-ack… that mania-a-ac."

The audience was good-spirited and laughed at our songs about Kuwait and Iraq, but we could sense that everyone knew our bombers were already airborne.

"Time to blow the whistle, time to send a missile to Iraq."

Around 9:00 PM, deadline time, we broke for intermission. News spread through the theater foyer that Saddam wasn't budging.

"Bomb bomb bomb, bomb bomb Iraq."

Thus began Operation Desert Storm-in Norman. One night later, on Wednesday evening, January 16, most of us were at home when the first streaks of Iraqi antiaircraft tracer fire lit up the moonless Baghdad sky. Some of us were watching TV—*Seinfeld* was on—when the networks broke in, preempting all programming for the rest of the night. (From your nightly Gomorrah, we now bring you…Saddam.) We all watched the tracer bullets over the eerie Baghdad skyline of minarets, domes, and dull concrete, listening to Peter Arnett's breathless reporting, wondering what to make of it all.

It was odd. It was real. It was mesmerizing. It was also, we decided, funny.

That hasn't always been so with America's wars. The Vietnam War produced jarringly few good jokes, and what little humor there was tended to be partisan, "dove" or "hawk." We can't imagine trying to get an audience to laugh at "both sides" of a war debate that ground on for nearly a decade. Vietnam was reputed to have been a killer of comedic careers. Not a single prominent satirist of the prewar years held on through and after the war. Stan Freberg went into advertising, Tom Lehrer into teaching, and who knows what Vaughn Meader did. A few comic shows arose during the war—like *The Smothers Brothers Comedy Hour* and Rowan and Martin's *Laugh-In*—and Mark Russell began his tenure in a little club on C Street, near the U.S. Capitol, but satirists had to struggle to be heard amid all the shouting and marching and yelling.

Vietnam fit a long-established pattern, through our history: unpopular wars aren't funny. Popular wars are—or, at least, they can be. Controversial clashes, like the Mexican-American War or Spanish-American War, produced no comic songs of note. The others, the big ones—the Revolution, the Civil War, and both World Wars—all did.

Measured joke for joke, punch lines versus chow lines, Operation Desert Storm was far and away the most amusing war in American history. Maybe in anybody's history.

Actually, the jokes had begun back in early August, the year before (1990), when Saddam Hussein surprised the world by making good on his threat to invade Kuwait if it didn't cut back its oil output. The global furor was immediate—and so was the comedy. Often, humorists will wait a few days before deciding whether to take on a military topic. Not this time. Right after Iraqi troops rolled into Kuwait City, America's airwaves bristled with jokes, some fresh, some clichéd (like how the U.S. was caught between Iraq and a hard place), some tasteful, some not. Disc jockeys later reported that, during the first month after the invasion, they received several dozen parody songs (including ours) by mail, many of them very funny.

Why so?

In part, people were ready to laugh because Kuwait appeared to be the utter anti-Vietnam. No jungles, hidden troops, secretive townspeople, or mixed loyalties. The geography was very simple. Thanks to the pancake desert (and new technology), you could know if the enemy was nearby. The main villain (Saddam) cast the figure of a comic jerk, not a wispy mystic (Ho Chi Minh). The stakes were clearer: more Americans drove cars than played dominos. The U.S. president was liked, not loathed, by younger people. There was no draft. The media provided us with celebrity personalities, not sober war correspondents.

Last but certainly not least for those of us in the business of parody, the name of the adversary lent itself to puns on dozens, maybe hundreds, of rock and roll songs. Iraq = I rock. Yes! One of our first songs, *"Iraq Is Robbin'"* (tweedle-ee-dee), a parody of "Rockin' Robin," rolled oh-so-naturally off our rock 'n roll–schooled lips.

Walt Disney's imagineers could not have invented a better comic foil than Saddam Hussein, pure meanness with a jaunty strut. Our performers played him simply, in a maroon beret and pea-green military jacket. The voice? A snarly baritone was good, but an evil bass was better. The attitude? Think of it as Steve Martin doing Groucho Marx doing Charlie Chaplin doing Hitler. That meant a cigar, even though we're not sure we've ever seen Saddam smoke one. And, of course, paste-on eyebrows and moustaches. For that, we used regular theatrical gaffer's tape, which often fell off from a sweaty upper lip, always good for an extra laugh. (Sometimes, our Saddams would blow through their nose and wiggle their lips to make it fall off to get that laugh.)

Our own leader, George Bush, who had not long before touchingly yearned for a "kind and gentle" land, had grown into Commander George, World War II hero, lips eminently readable, madder than we'd ever seen him except when he'd lent his son Neil all that S&L money. His New World Order had developed a new weird odor. The last time Bush had taken a stand this strong was back in March 1990, when he'd declared, "I'm president of the United States, and I'm not going to eat any more broccoli." When he said it, he meant it, in a thinly disguised message to anyone anywhere who meant the U.S. and its allies any harm.

"This will not stand," the president told Saddam, mispronouncing it as *Sahd*-um, instead of Suh-*Dahm*. According to rumor, he intended this as a squirrelly insult, because *Sahd*-um, in some obscure Middle Eastern tongue, translates into "shoeshine boy."

Bush was aptly aided by two modern macho generals, Colin Powell and "Stormin'" Norman Schwarzkopf, the kind of hero-brand brass we all remembered from the old black-and-white World War II movies—you know, the ones who would summon John Wayne into their spartan offices, lower their chins, and speak gravely about how and why we would win this thing. And, for sheer toughness, grizzled courage, and all those other traditional masculine virtues, we had the State Department press aide Margaret Tutwiler squarely on our side.

Then there were the media heartthrobs. Unlike Vietnam, Desert Storm took place in a new world of twenty-four-hour TV news channels, and anchors turned into celebrities. We could imagine love-starved women tuning in at all hours, in hopes of seeing yet another desperate report from eye-candy Scud Stud Arthur Kent silhouetted against the breaking dawn, gentle explosions in the background, in his slightly sweaty, stylishly unbuttoned battle shirt, telling us he'd been advised to run for cover but first wanted to share his feelings from the zone of danger.

★★★★★★★★★★★★★★★★
16 Funniest Objects, U.S. History
1. Monica Lewinsky's blue dress
2. Richard Nixon's tapes
3. Warren Harding's closet
4. Joe McCarthy's hearings
5. Lorena Bobbitt's knife
6. Andrew Jackson's muddy boots
7. Bill Clinton's boxers and briefs
8. George Bush Sr.'s lips
9. Bob Packwood's diary
10. Abraham Lincoln's stovepipe hat
11. Al Gore's sighs
12. Richard Nixon's plumbers
13. Benjamin Franklin's almanac
14. Ken Starr's report
15. Dan Quayle's grades
16. Jimmy Carter's killer rabbit

The real source of entertainment, at the home front, came from the gas pump. The only thing faster than the troop deployment was the speed at which gas stations were raising prices. The biggest run-up occurred in late 1990, no doubt adding to the popularity of the troop buildup. Unlike in Jimmy Carter's day, these were no mere human beings we were trying to save. This was oil. We sang "Tie a Yellow Ribbon 'Round My Oldsmobile" to audiences that were tying yellow ribbons all over the place to honor the troops while at the same time hanging onto their gas guzzlers. ("We saved Kuwait / For daddy's V-8.")

Adding to the fun, the army rolled out the Humvee (with a roof-mounted gun) and Hummer (base model), each of which required all the oil of a small Arab nation just to make one round-trip to and from the front lines. So, in early January 1991, thanks to the good offices of Exxon, Gulf, Mobil, and Texaco, those proud servants of public interest, the U.S. House and Senate voted (by very narrow margins) to authorize Bush to use force to drive Iraq from Kuwait.

To Saddam, the looming conflict was to be the "mother of all battles," even if, to our fighting forces, he himself was a mother-something-else. On one side were the Revolutionary Guards. On the other, were the forces of the Great Satan. With help from the United Nations, the U.S. had assembled a magnificent thirty-nine-nation fighting force. Saddam quaked with fear with the knowledge that troops from Singapore, Senegal, Sweden, Honduras, Bangladesh, and (cringe) France and Italy—history's two most fabled military powers—were lining up against him. One small detail about the thirty-nine-nation force: 70 percent came from one nation. Unfortunately for Saddam, it wasn't Italy.

TRACK: 20

★★★★★★★★★★★★★★★★★

Bomb Bomb Iraq
(parody of "Barbara Ann")

Kurd kurd kurd, kurd is the word,
    a well a
Kurd kurd kurd, kurd is the word,
    a well a...
Bomb bomb bomb, bomb bomb Iraq
Bomb bomb bomb, bomb bomb Iraq
Let's bomb Ira-a-aq
Bomb bomb bomb, bomb bomb Iraq
Yeah, let's atta-a-ack that mania-a-ac
I think it's time we blow the whistle
Don't you fire a missile on Iraq
Bomb bomb, bomb bomb
Ka-boom!

We couldn't help but notice a "Mouse that Roared" sort of charm to a square-off between what appeared to be the entire intergalactic solar system and one nutcake of a little country. Camel Lot. (Where things go *bam!* a lot.) Mesopotamia. The hanging gardens of Babylon. It's just like the ancient Iraqi joke: "I'm OK, Ur OK."

Amid the snarl, one even smaller nation tried its best to remain neutral, as if it could pass as the Switzerland of the Middle East. No, it wasn't Afghanistan. (You can look it up: they were part of the coalition.) It was Israel.

American leaders spent a lot of time convincing virtually every *other* nation in the world to become involved and join our coalition, but gingerly suggested to Israel to lie low—everyone knew its involvement would raise the stakes. "Won't you stay home, Israelis," we sang. And since Japan wasn't sticking its neck out, to say the least, we had an easy rhyme: "Israelis won't you please…be like the Japanese!" In the end, Israel stayed home, but Saddam's scuds sure didn't. Meanwhile, we were "looking for scuds in all the wrong places."

The air war lasted six weeks, and set the stage for the ground war. Saddam thought we were going to attack along the coast, but we sure tricked him by invading inland and attacking his rear, the largest tank advance since Henry Fonda squared off against Robert Shaw in *The Battle of the Bulge*. Stormin' Norman called it his "Hail Mary" play, but it reminded us of one of those hidden hand-off plays where the blockers go one way and the runner another. Except this play didn't produce a touchdown. With the goal line (Baghdad) in sight, we laid the ball down on the one-yard line, where Saddam flopped on it. Then came the one-hundred-hour whistle.

War over. Everybody go home.

The war ended so quickly, the paint was barely dry on our tank props.

Trying to put on a comedy act in the midst of those one hundred hours of actual shooting, killing, and dying did raise a few eyebrows, but what were we to do? Our audiences were a tad more quiet than before, and we shaved a few numbers and rewrote a few lines, but people still found it amusing. When peace came, on February 27, we went back to our old ways.

So did Saddam. Big surprise. The least gracious loser since Tonya Harding, he set fire to more than seven hundred Kuwaiti oil wells, prompting our "Oil in the World" sing-along song (remember "Jeremiah the Bullfrog"?). We had more than a little difficulty reenacting a 26,000-square-mile fire on a cabaret stage.

In the end, Desert Storm was a boon for many people. CNN rode a ratings bonanza. New media superstars were born. The price of gas went down again. Bush's popularity ratings went through the ceiling (for about ten minutes). The veterans came home to ticker-tape parades.

Six months after the war ended, we were invited by the White House to present a show in the East Room, at the exact same spot where many wartime presidential announcements had been made. Bush's staff asked us to go easy on him. "It's been a rough year," one of them told Bill Strauss. "Lay off the boss." We swallowed our objections and prepared a twenty-minute program of nine songs that said not one word about Bush. Half the cabinet was there, along with most of the Bush family, Marilyn and Dan Quayle, and assorted other family and political friends. So we sang about Saddam, and Wolf Blitzer, and Barbara—we even did "Millie the Poocher" (apologies to Cab Calloway) in front of the First Pooch herself. ("Hide de hide de bone.") But we made no jokes whatsoever at the president's expense. At the end of the show, our Guest-in-Chief interrupted our bows, came up to the stage, and asked us, "Has this show been censored?"

To which Bill replied that, yes, it had been.

Whereupon we received a firm order, from the leader of the free world, to do our Desert Storm songs about him.

TRACK: 21

★★★★★★★★★★★★★★★★

Tie a Yellow Ribbon 'Round My Oldsmobile (parody of "Tie a Yellow Ribbon 'Round the Old Oak Tree")

Troops are comin' home, I think it's nice
But don't expect that I will sacrifice
I thank those desert soldiers and that military brass
For guardin' what we cherish in the U.S. middle class
Our right to guzzle gas
I'll tie a yellow ribbon 'round my Oldsmobile
Watch me burn that oil
Hear my tires squeal
At six miles to the gallon
In my hot wide-trackin' wheels
We saved Kuwait
For daddy's V-8
Seven tons of steel
I'll try some mellow livin' in my souped-up Oldsmobile

By then, we knew all too well what destruction had befallen the last miniature army that had disobeyed a Bush order. So we saluted crisply and did as told. We made the right choice. Ten years have passed, since we dealt with Bush on his terms. He lost his next election, but we're still in business.

8

Culture War Chic
("Multipetaled Victims of Pesticidal Food Chain Chauvinism")

★★★★★★★★★
TRACKS: 22–24

"Reds / Time to stop the Stalin, those days are gone / Reds / When they speak of Lenin, they now mean John / They want to be like we are / Perfect in every way / Oh, what's the matter with Reds today?"

While we sang this parody of "Kids," first the Berlin Wall and then the Soviet Union collapsed in a world that had room for only two bona fide superpowers: the Cowboys and the 49ers.

As satirists, we had felt this coming. Through the '80s, it seemed like every other month we'd wake up to news that some Soviet premier had just died. While the rest of the world was wondering *What does this mean for history?*, our warped minds were deciphering What rhymes with Andropov? Chernenko?

★★★★★★★★★★★★★★★★

**Like a Suburban Drone
(parody of "Like a Rolling Stone")**

Oh, thirty years ago, you felt a hurt,
    wore a tie-dye shirt
Slept in the dirt, didn't you
People used to shout, an' say watch out
You're bound to sell out
But you thought that they were all...
    kiddin' you
But now you find it ... hard to explain
Why you still hum the tunes of the
    Jefferson Airplane
Now you warn your teenage kid
Do like you say, but don't do like you did
While you tell 'em, don't get naked in
    my hot tub
So how does it feel?
Tell me how does it feel?
To be a wealthy man
Who drives a minivan
And has a 401-K plan
A Republican

Gorbachev? ("Hottest red since Andropov / He's the world's first yuppie slav.")

With *glasnost* and *perestroika* in full swing, our audiences no longer wanted to laugh at funny songs about nuclear destruction, they now wanted songs about funny-hip Russians. ("Forget your rubles, c'mon, get preppie / Give your red up for pink an' green / Forget your troubles, you're feelin' peppie / We're goin' down to L.L. Bean.")

Boris Yeltsin climbed atop a tank—and didn't vow to bury us, only to outdrink us. Our performers tried to one-up each other with their tipsy Boris pratfalls, until one show in New York's Houseman Theater, when Brad Van Grack fell into the first row and dislocated his shoulder right at the close of Act One. We had to drag him offstage, call an ambulance, and pretend that it was "All part of the show, ladies and gentlemen, all part of the show."

With the U.S. now atop the global pecking order, Americans were agog over multilateralism. Academicians were busy popping out "End of History" essays that were brilliant (but wrong), and the U.S. Congress couldn't restrain itself with its glee that the nation's shores would never again require defending. A decade earlier, in the very earliest months of the Capitol Steps, we had put together a Senate hearing on useless military properties. Now, at long last, some of those properties were getting sold. ("I've grown accustomed to this base... / Its golf, its sports, its tennis courts are second nature to me now.")

Yes, the cold war was officially over, and the global beer was definitely getting warm. But something was missing.

Sure, Bush's "New World Order" made life kind and gentle, but around the globe, the old entertainment value was missing. Watching world news was kind of like watching a football game with only one team. A touchdown pass is only thrilling when someone is trying to smash the quarterback and stomp the receiver.

Even the Olympics weren't as much fun as before. There was nobody nasty to root against (except maybe the global megacorporations, whose logos were now bigger than the shrinking flags on athletes' jerseys).

Americans needed enemies. Desperately.

For an easy team to beat, we could have picked the Italians. But instead, we chose each other. With no war even remotely in sight anywhere else in the world, we started one right here at home.

We started a Culture War.

We didn't want to argue about big things, like money. No. Our chattering classes, left and right, shared their faith in go-go gimme-gimme economics through which they could cash in on their TV face time and get rich.

Instead, we wanted to argue about little things. Like children—and all the little things we stuffed in, dumped on, and wrapped around our tykes. Like movies, music, TV, books, clothing, tattoos, body piercings, and other essentials of modern youth.

The Culture War had two sides. One side consisted of evil bible-toting, sex-obsessed, chip-munching, cigar-smoking, tree-chopping, school-ruining, child-destroying dittoheads. The other side had the evil porn-toting, sex-obsessed, granola-munching, pot-smoking, tree-hugging, school-ruining, child-destroying feminazis. The two sides utterly loathed one another, which—once you read their fundraising literature—was quite understandable.

Culture War Right had its '80s-era origins in Ron and Nancy Reagan, Ed Meese, and Phyllis Schlafley. By the late '80s, Jim and Tammy Faye Bakker's PTL Ministry really popped open the comedic can, and within a few years the humor scene was peopled by over-the-top reverends like Jerry Falwell and Pat Robertson (talking with God—*that's* entertainment) and all the Rush Limbaughs, Bill Bennetts, and think tankers, sanctimonious authors, and assorted extraneous cause-meisters. The many Americans who loathe that list of names must admit that, by way of compensation, their erstwhile foes have provided ample punchlines in their even ampler corduroys.

Culture Wars Left also dished up more than its share of punchlines. Recall William Kennedy Smith and Uncle Ted, putting Palm Beach on the humor map.

Lending paunch to the raunch, we joined Senator Kennedy with Senator Joseph Biden in a Gilbert & Sullivan "Ruler of the Queen's Na-Vee" parody we entitled, "The Rulers of Morality" ("Let's check her assiduity / If it's firm enough, I'll let her work for me").

Hollywood's denizens of cool were often funnier than their own scripts. ("People / People who make sequels / Are the yuckiest people in the world.") Our own D.C. mayor, Marion Barry, became a famous conscientious objector in the War on Drugs. ("I've been lookin' for drugs in all the wrong places.") Doctor Koop, who was busy promoting safe sex, himself starred in our "Little Deuce Coupe" parody ("Said the little Doc Koop / You don't know what she's got…") on our second PBS special.

Senate nomination fights gave all America a glimpse of left-right cleavage—where, previously, men of both camps were frequently known to look down on that. Judge Bork's "borking" wasn't much fun. He seemed way too grumpy to get giggles, and besides, we comedians were already in Gomorrah, not just limping there—but Clarence Thomas was a laugh riot, with his lurid tales of "Long Dong Silver" and pubic hairs on Coke cans. Having been Senate staffers ourselves, we could easily picture committee investigators poring over Thomas's proclivities for dirty talk and porno films. Anita Hill was funny too, with her earnest descriptions of how Clarence had treated her so horribly she felt compelled to follow him from one job to another. Part of what made that story so entertaining was the mystery of this classic "he says, she says" love-affair-turned-hate-affair. Which of the two told the truth? Maybe both, maybe neither. We didn't care, and our jokes didn't take sides. Neither did our audiences. All they did was laugh, at Clarence and Anita both.

We had to take some care with that tale, given the great taboo of political satire: race. That's always a tough issue for a comedian of any color to handle. But we tried, because we had to stay atop the news when the news turned racial.

We mooched David Duke and gibed the Simi Valley jury that acquitted the cops in the Rodney King case, but the closest we ever got to a racial joke was our satire of the Oakland, California, School Board's new "ebonics" program. To the alphabet song, in a sketch we called "Hooked on Ebonics," we sang "A B C B I B U B He B She Be They Be, ba-bee!" But when a (mostly) Caucasian group jokes about race, it's a mandatory rule to twist the final punch line against your Anglo-Saxon ancestry. So we spun that routine out with "Hooked on Dweebonics" ("A-drive, B-drive, CD-Rom, E-mail, F-key, GIF, HTTP teleport, IBM retry-abort") and Hooked on Moronics ("I mean, like it's A, then, is it, B, then, you know, C, and then, as if, it's like a G, and then Q, and then, um, and it's W for, like, *what*ever").

Through our performing era, it's been way more acceptable for minorities to make jokes about whites than vice-versa. In some ways, this can be seen as one of history's even-uppers, given that there was such a long period of time when the reverse was true—when whites constantly depicted minorities as inferiors, and minorities would have risked life and limb by taking comic swipes at whites.

Jokes about other nonwhite ethnic groups—and about immigrants—are just as risky, taste-wise. We avoid making fun of accents, hair styles, or ethnic mannerisms unless we're referring to foreigners. One particularly rowdy ethnic song, "Euro Pest," is one of our all-time crowd pleasers. Why? Because it's about the French. Maybe it's because France is the one other nation in the world whose smugness exceeds ours—but, whatever the reason, glaciers will cover the Congo before the French ever get any protection in the Culture War.

Cleverly co-written by Mike Tilford, this parody of the *Beauty and the Beast* "Be Our Guest" song lampoons the initial financial woes of France's EuroDisney amusement park by presenting two nasty, smelly, raunchy Frenchmen in mouse ears, singing ("Don't ask me for *bonjours* / *En France* Mickey says 'up yours' / Wait on you? You must be joking / Go away, I'm busy smoking / I spit out your brioche / Go away, I never wash"). Sing lines like that about other ethnic groups, and you'll get calls from reporters, lawyers, and EEOC officials. Sing them about the French, and you'll get laughs.

You have to trust your audience. When you tell a joke, you can tell if people like it. If they don't think it's tasteful, you can hear that too.

★★★★★★★★★★★★★★★★
16 FUNNIEST OBJECTS, WORLD HISTORY

1. Mao's *Little Red Book*
2. Marie Antoinette's cake
3. Emperor Nero's fiddle
4. Henry VIII's wedding vows
5. King Tut's tomb
6. Stonehenge
7. Napoleon's clothes
8. The Sphinx
9. Boris Yeltsin's tank
10. Machu Picchu
11. The Spanish Armada
12. The Great Wall of China
13. Russia's nuclear safeguards
14. England's mad cows
15. Hanging gardens of Babylon
16. Ponce de Leon's fountain of youth

TRACK: 23

★ ★

You Don't Bring Me Floriculturally Diverse Polyfragrant Soilistically Challenged Multipetaled Victims of Pesticidal Food Chain Chauvinism
(parody of "You Don't Bring Me Flowers")

MAN
I can't bring you flowers
WOMAN
You can't sing me love songs
MAN
I don't try to talk anymore, since each word
   has to be —
WOMAN
Nonsexist, nonracist, nonheterosexist, postfeminist,
   multiculturalist, secular humanist, environmentalist,
   and 100 percent free of the slightest trace
   of Eurocentricity
MAN
I remember when I'd treat you like my honey
WOMAN
You'd treat me like the victim of institutionalized pat-
   terns of discrimination against women, gays, Aleutian
   Islanders, spotted owls, and laboratory bunnies
MAN
I don't sort all my trash into twelve garbage pails
I don't spend every weekend out saving the whales
And I read lots of books by those old
Dead white males
Shakespeare will be ...

WOMAN
Bard
MAN
Forevermore
We male chauvinist pigs once could always get kissed
Now our species is on the endangerment list
If we can't find a mate, we'll die out and be missed
WOMAN
Msss-ed
MAN
Extinct just like the giant dinosaur
WOMAN
This male chauvinist pig I must love and protect
For to love endangered species is
Politically correct
You can bring me ...
MAN
Floriculturally diverse, polyfragrant, soilistically
   challenged multipetaled victims of
   pesticidical food chain chauvinism
WOMAN
You can bring me flowers
Evermore

It's too facile to blame "political correctness" for this limit on our public sense of humor. There are good reasons why anyone in the business of comedy needs to show a little restraint on issues of this kind.

If mishandled, humor can be yet another form of power, through which a dominant group can intimidate the others. This is currently still true for race—let's hope, not so long from now, it won't be—but it's also true about income class, nationality, and age. If a rich person jokes about the habits and misfortunes of poor people, that risks being offensive far more than if a poor person jokes about the habits and misfortunes of the rich. (To the tune of "Matilda"—"Mike Milken / He took de money / And go to de jaila."). As Mark Eaton puts it, "Seeing a business man in a $700 suit slip and fall in the mud is always funnier than some regular guy in jeans getting muddy."

Similarly, for years we parodied "Teach Your Children Well," poking fun at the old living in Sun Cities off our FICA money ("Tax our children well / To pay for swell / Old age adventures / It's you we're living off / So we can golf / And buy our dentures"). That worked well enough among people our age, but not always so well among older people. Sometimes one of our cast members would see a cute elderly couple sitting in the front row and return backstage asking to cut that song.

Generational jokes have been a core aspect of the Culture War, in part because one can trace so much of that war's festering arguments to those crazy campuses of the 1960s. Many baby boomers have an unrequitable obsession with replaying the old '60s dormroom debates endlessly, left and right.

In the early '80s, we covered the boomer transition from hippie to stockbroker with songs like "Momma, Don't Let Your Babies Grow Up to be Yuppies." The core joke on boomers then, as always, was the amazing depth and breadth of their hypocrisies. Boomers had become adults (a word we use here guardedly) who thought they could *do* anything they wanted, as long as they *felt right* about it. The relevance to the Culture War was this: to a typical boomer, one's own behavior matters not a whit, as long as one holds the correct position on the issues.

By the late '80s, boomers were well established with houses, lawns, kids, and pets, inspiring Richard Paul to write and perform a parody of "Like a Rolling Stone." Entitled "Like a Suburban Drone," Richard portrayed a brooding, aging, snarling Bob Dylan at a time the real Dylan remained aloof, unsure what to be, do, or say in this new era. ("Oh, once upon a time you felt a hurt, wore a tie-dye shirt, slept in the dirt /

Didn' you? / People used to shout, you better watch out, you're bound to sell out, but you thought that they were all / Kiddin' you.")

The song was an immediate hit—and, in time, a classic—capturing a new cultural hipness that was, foremost and first, an inquiry into feelings, as in mine, yours, his, hers, its, theirs, *everybody's*. ("So how does it feel / Yeah, tell me how does it feel?") Along with a new comfort with hypocrisy, we no longer were Dylan's "like a complete unknown." Now, our anxieties were shifting with the new mood ("To have a cellular phone / And a colonial home / Like a suburban drone"). When Richard performed this song, boomer women in the crowd would poke their husbands with recognition.

In the early '90s, when Gen X emerged on the cultural scene, we brought the boomers' generational narcissism into the lyrics. ("You're so distressed by Generation X / You don't like their backwards caps, young girls dancin' on guys' laps, and havin' sex / Remember sex?") By this point, many boomers had teenagers to worry about, as well. ("You used to hang out in People's Park / Now when you see kids get stoned, you want to call a narc.") Not to mention their own reputations ("No pot, you've turned the page, you stick with booze / You're deep in middle age, you got too much to lose").

Yet, even in deep middle age, with wallets growing as wide as their pants and the old "Summer of Love" nothing more than a website (www.summeroflove.com), even boomers have feelings. ("So how does it feel? / Yeah, tell me how does it feel? / To be a wealthy man / Who drives a minivan / And has a 401-K plan / A Republican, oooh.")

Gender jokes are far easier, thanks perhaps to the recent leveling of the comedic playing field there. Before Lucille Ball, nearly all American comic performers, and comic writers, were male. In recent decades, we've seen vast progress here. Even if we've yet to see a woman president, our country is awash in funny female performers and writers.

For twenty years, the Capitol Steps have been run by a woman and man (your two authors), and we've pulled no punches in the gender trenches of the Culture War. We've whacked all manner of macho males, conservative or liberal, in dozens of songs and sketches. We've tried to cover *real* feminist issues, like liberating Ladies Room lines in theaters. We've carved up humorless lefty man-haters with a wicked bit, "Angry

Feminist Nursery Rhymes," about a Women's Study professor. ("Little Ms. Muffett sat on her tuffett / Eating her curds and whey / Along came a spider who sat down beside her / Which Ms. Muffett squished with her birkenstock.") And, in one of our all-time favorite songs, we parodied "You Can Bring Me Flowers" with "You Can Bring Me Floriculturally Diverse, Polyfragrant, Soilistically Challenged, Multipetaled Victims of Pesticidical Food Chain Chauvinism."

Here, obviously, we played off the new linguistic fun Culture War Left was providing the nation. Every noun, verb, adjective, and adverb in the English language now had to render tender mercies to the oh-so-oppressed. In the People's Republic of China, they've done this through torture at reeducation camps. In America, up to this point, the main punishment has been the denial of sexual opportunity by instructors, mostly women, to language-abusers, mostly men. The corrective device, recognizable as the frosty glare, has been administered at seminars, conventions, executive retreats, and other places where aging boomers go to network, or, as younger people would say, to hook up.

In our song, a modern boomer man at such an event tries to maneuver around the frosty glares of a modern boomer woman by skillfully adapting to her vocabulary. ("A waiter or waitress is now a waitron / That means Trinidad now must be called Trinitron.") Gradually, like so many millions of hunter-gatherers before him, our man learned how to gather in his hunt, by snaring his prey in her own trap. ("We male chauvinist pigs once could always get kissed / Now our species is on the endangerment list / If we can't find a mate, we'll die out and be missed / Extinct just like the giant dinosaur.") This modern woman, being so exquisitely attuned to every *cause du jour*, simply cannot allow any endangered species to die, and is obliged to accept his entreaties—and his flowers ("a pistil and a stamen," which he reminds her are "a pistil and a stayperson"), and all ends well.

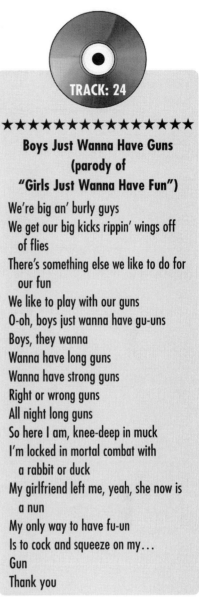

TRACK: 24

★★★★★★★★★★★★★★★★

Boys Just Wanna Have Guns (parody of "Girls Just Wanna Have Fun")

We're big an' burly guys
We get our big kicks rippin' wings off of flies
There's something else we like to do for our fun
We like to play with our guns
O-oh, boys just wanna have gu-uns
Boys, they wanna
Wanna have long guns
Wanna have strong guns
Right or wrong guns
All night long guns
So here I am, knee-deep in muck
I'm locked in mortal combat with a rabbit or duck
My girlfriend left me, yeah, she now is a nun
My only way to have fu-un
Is to cock and squeeze on my...
Gun
Thank you

Why is this song still popular with audiences, long after all the fuss about political correctness has died down? It's partly because the English language is a font for humor, especially at its ever-shifting frontiers. But it's also because, no matter how deep the Culture War, and no matter what our ticket to it—left, right, white, black, native, immigrant, rich, poor, old, young, male, female—we're all human beings who know this: when the day is done, each of us needs a little hug. And a little laugh.

The Cold War came and went. So will the Culture War. To get through things like these, it doesn't hurt to cool our jets, keep some perspective, and show a sense of humor.

9

The Joy of Sax
("Why Not Take Al and Me?")

★★★★★★★★
TRACKS: 25–28

One of the most enjoyable trips the Capitol Steps ever took was in 1986 to Little Rock, Arkansas. When we arrived, we walked into a party for fat-cat Democratic donors where we had a fine time, feted by a tall gangly guy with a shuffly walk, scruffy light brown hair, and coy grin.

We'd met a number of governors in our first half dozen years of shows, but this Arkansan was easily the chummiest, and the most, well, like *us*. On the fly, we wrote a song about some lowbrow political rival of his, and he laughed and laughed. His wife wasn't around, and he flirted a little with the women on our cast—nothing much, all in fun, just being friendly.

That was the first time the Capitol Steps met Bill Clinton.

A couple years later, in 1988, our young governor friend gave a dreadfully dull and long-winded speech at the Democratic National Convention. We tried to roast him with a Billy Joel parody, "I Will Be Talking for the Longest Time," to not many laughs, because Clinton hadn't made the national joke radar. We ditched the song and assumed that was the last we and the nation would hear of him.

Wrong.

Our paths wouldn't cross again, comedically, until the 1992 New Hampshire primary season, at a pre-election show in Manchester. At the State Theater, there was a huge crush for tickets, with scalpers, even. It figured. The local airwaves were full of attack ads, political signs were everywhere, and, we figured, half the homes in the state had some candidate sleeping on a living room sofa.

Up to that point, "The Tsounds of Tsongas" was our hit of the season (along with any song that featured Dan Quayle). But as the election approached, an old Clinton flame named Gennifer Flowers told some tales, the nation met Hillary in her sly "I'm no Tammy Wynette" mode, and Bill bit his lip and gave his semi-sort-of apology on *60 Minutes.* The huge crowd laughed at everything that night, but they utterly roared at anything about Clinton.

Laughter is a form of polling, as anyone who tells political jokes for a living can vouch. If you're a candidate who gets no laughs at all, that's the worst. That probably means no one knows who you are. If you get drooling, gut-hurting, crying and pointing laughter, that's not so good, either (ask Bob Packwood). There are laughters of different depth and breadth, fading and shading, attitude and latitude. If you're a candidate, you want people laughing *with* you, not at you. But the very best kind of laugh is what Clinton got that night, the laughter of self-recognition. People like to laugh at themselves—and many in our audience saw more than a little of their own foibles in Clinton's personal mischief-making.

SIXTEEN SCANDALS

A few days later, he won that primary. Actually, he finished second to Tsongas in the actual vote count, but his spinners persuaded the media that "The Comeback Kid" was coming back, so chalk that as a win. Onward and upward he went, through the rest of the primaries—Super Tuesday, New York, California. Week by week, we added more Clinton material in the show, presenting him as Elvis, equal parts hip cat and hound dog, a little smart and a little sexy, very much a dry and light good-cellar '69 vintage *Chateau de Woodstock* boomer. A guy from our old late-night dorm parties, a smart and hip draft-dodging Georgetown-*cum*-Yalie with an equally hip and smart Wellesley-cum-Yalie wife. Together, they took on the world, working it, charming it, and fooling it. Now, only in their mid-forties, Bill and Hill were on the brink of the ultimate political achievement. How better to cement it than to pick a running mate tandem, Al and Tipper Gore, of the same vintage, same style, same baby boomer everything?

We liked that. A delicious prospect presented itself: after doing this show for eleven years, we finally got to pick on people our own age (other than Dan Quayle, but *that* was too easy).

Bill Strauss felt a particular kinship, having been Al Gore's classmate at Harvard, and having known him through Bill's *Generations* book-writing project. He and Al shared similar views about many things, including what their boomer peers were looking for in leaders. Al felt his first run in 1988 was done in, partly, by a little generational envy among a group who, given the chance, might end up in a seventy-million-way tie for the presidency, with each boomer voting for him- or herself.

Al struck us as a fun kind of guy who, had he been born to any dad other than a U.S. Senator, might have ended up a Congressional staffer—and Capitol Stepper—himself. Twice before the '92 campaign, Al had joined us on stage, and both times he displayed real potential as a professional comic—once as "Prince Albert of Gore" in our *Shamlet* skit, once as our introducer. We had urged him to be funny, and he sure grabbed hold of the moment, delivering our stock lines, some of his own, and a few ad libs with perfect timing and facial expression.

Our generation had gone mainstage in more than just politics, and wisps of gray were creeping into our temples. We weren't the young comedians on the block any more. When we began, we ranged in age from twenty-two to thirty-four. Now our ages ranged from the mid-thirties to mid-forties. Most of our new cast members were married. Many of us had children. Everyone knows boomers have always occupied the middle of the universe, from birth forward. Now we also stood at the middle of the life cycle—hence our kinship with two like-aged guys seeking out the highest offices in the land.

One of our hot pre-election songs, "Al and Me," a parody of "All of Me," gibed the clear connection the Clinton/Gore bus tour was making with voters in our audience. ("Make some room for sensitive boomers / We're havin' fun / Aboard Greyhound One / We're ridin' on Trailways / We're bondin' in male ways / How far can two bus boys go?") The songs we were still singing about Bush, to fewer laughs, convinced us long before the polls closed that this race was going Clinton's way.

If you can believe this, we'd had such a good run with the Bush Sr./Dan Quayle administration that we were actually rooting *against* Bill Clinton in 1992. We were upset at trading Quayle for Gore. As Jim Aidala put it, they "owed us two first-round draft picks."

By now, the Capitol Steps had shed our mostly centrist Republican origins, and our personal link to the Congress was loosening. In the early '90s, we let go of our old rule requiring new cast members to be full-time Capitol Hill staffers. We did ask performers to do Capitol Hill internships, although back then "intern" was not a punchline. From 1992 through Clinton's first term, we acquired several new performers who didn't know a markup from make-up, but who sure knew how to sing and play funny characters.

On that 1992 election night, more than a few Steppers were sad to see our friend George, and our profit-center Dan, leave the public stage. But even those among us who had not voted for Clinton realized, when the Clintons and Gores shared those hugs on election night, our generation now bore the mantle of the power elite *and* culture elite.

We had a lot of shows in the days right before and after the November 1992 general election, and we had to evolve our material as fast as Clinton evolved his persona—as in, daily. We assigned him to our best rock 'n roll singers. For costume, we settled on a modified Elvis look, in black leather and shades, with a golden sax on a sling, topped by a poodlish wig. "The Joy of Sax" was set to "Jailhouse Rock."

("Mister Willie's playin' on his saxophone / Hillary can run the country on her own / The whole dang government we'll reinvent / An' Al Gore's lookin' most excellent / Let's rock…")

We played him plump, a fast-food addict, the Lord of the Fries. ("You can't hide those giant thighs / He likes burgers, shakes, and fries.") Where *Saturday Night Live* portrayed Clinton as not above stealing french fries from children during campaign stops, we advertised Clinton's enormous thighs as "the other white meat."

★★★★★★★★★★★★★★★
16 Funniest Presidents, U.S. History
1. Bill Clinton
2. Richard Nixon
3. John Kennedy
4. Millard Fillmore
5. Teddy Roosevelt
6. Andrew Jackson
7. George Washington
8. Harry Truman
9. Grover Cleveland
10. George H.W. Bush
11. John Adams
12. Gerald Ford
13. George W. Bush
14. Thomas Jefferson
15. Herbert Hoover
16. Ronald Reagan

And, of course, there was That Face. Where Reagan had been uncannily skilled at posture and body, bringing to mind the movie greats in classic westerns, Clinton knew how to use every muscle in his face. He must have watched a lot of *Days of Our Lives* and *As the World Turns*, because he sure got that soap attitude down and dirty.

All our Clinton character had to do was walk on stage, pause, wiggle a little, bite a lip, lift up a Ray-Ban and wink at a lady at a front table with a little "Hi there," and everybody laughed. Our Clinton, like the real Clinton, was a player, a Dennis the Menace all grown up and grown out, the kind of rake you love to hate, or hate to love, or hate to hate, or love to love— whatever your opinion of him, you had to admit that the man filled any room he entered, real fast.

One of the many fun parts of doing live comedy on stage is that there are so many attractive people of the other gender in the first few rows (beyond that, you know they're there but can't see them) who are fixated on you, eyes wide, big smiles on their faces. To be able to answer back, in script and gesture—as our Clintons have for nearly ten years now— gives life to a performer's fantasy. "Hi there to you, and you, and you— and you over there, too." Oh, yeah. The many male Steppers who couldn't play Clinton had ample cause for envy.

In those heady six months, from the election through the new president's first one hundred days, we gave everything Clinton did, from tax

TRACK: 26

★★★★★★★★★★★★★★★★

**Ol' Whitewater Keeps on Rollin'
(parody of "Ol' Black Water")**

CLINTON
Well, I put down some grand on some
  Arkansas land
My lawyers tell me, I won't go to jail
When I'm alibi-ing
I'm not really lying
It's just that I'm trying
To never inhale
LAWYERS
Ol' Whitewater keeps on rollin'
CLINTON
I'm sick of all this talk about Whitewater
LAWYERS
Ol' Whitewater keeps on rollin'
CLINTON
And all these mean rumors about Hillary
LAWYERS
Ol' Whitewater keeps on rollin'
CLINTON
Hillary would never do anything immoral
Frankly, that's why I had to go to all those
  other women

hikes to arms talks, a sexual nuance. That, joined with the man's proclivity for shading the truth—from the draft to his eating habits to "I did not inhale"—rendered him a tomcat on the prowl worthy of a punch line to almost any joke you could write. Our performer, Porter Koontz, crafted his Clinton as "just so cocky and full of fun, kind of like the kid in school who always started the trouble but never got caught."

We usually started Clinton out with a few mock phone calls, on the news of the day, followed by a song. Among the many good things about Slick Willie, from the comic's perspective, was how you could ad lib all you wanted while staying quick to the character, because you could always bring it back to what was deep inside, which was: absolutely anything, this or that, everything or nothing. At one show, Porter entered as Clinton, and when keyboardist Howard Breitbart accidentally kicked out the electric cord on the piano and announced that he had no power, Porter's Clinton replied "That's OK, I don't have any power either."

His early administration had a "when will he clean up his room?" uniquely baby boomer kind of disarray. This began with don't-ask-don't-tell policy on gays in the military, which prompted for us the first of what would become many "Sound Off" routines, led by Major Disaster and General Confusion. Next came the very amusing selection of one female Attorney General after another, who each ran afoul of nanny laws, FICA taxes, child-care problems, and high-minded Senators. As we sang "Day Care" to "Day-O," the women in our audiences appreciated their new status as super-moms. This led, of course, to "The Middle-Aged Lady Named Janet Reno," a big-guy-in-drag who became a staple in our show. To this panoply came the ill-fated surgeon general, Jocelyn Elders—how could anybody be too kinky for *this* president?—and we had the best and funniest female cast of characters in the history of the American body politic.

And that didn't even include Hillary—even before all the scandals. We enjoyed Hillary's doomed-from-the-start effort to reform American health care, which we satirized with two stooge-like doctors in "You can suture yourself at home / Suture yourself in front of your family," culminating in our Hillary coming on the scene and barking instructions. Keyed only by a pert blonde wig—although back then she changed her hairstyle almost daily, driving our costumer mad—our Hillaries tried less to look or talk like the first lady than to reveal the steel of the inner her, with a brisk walk, active arms, and songs sung gleefully through clenched teeth.

Meanwhile, our black-wigged Gore got stiffer and stiffer and—these being the Clinton years, maybe we should stop there. His best entrance came on a wheeled dolly. Richard Paul played him as a dead man walking, Brian Ash as a mannequin, Jamie Zemeral as a robot, Mike Carruthers as a cross between the scarecrow and tinman of Oz. Great comedy can arise when you take two prisms that work OK on their own terms, but don't when combined—as with the concepts "dance" and "Al Gore." In 1994, at Al's (and our Bill's) twenty-fifth class reunion at Harvard, a body-painted hippie Bill persuaded a suit-coated Al to dance with him onstage, while Al pled to his classmates, per the Beatles, "Help me if you can, 'cuz I can't da-a-ance." That produced an enormous eruption of laughter from nearly a thousand of Al's and Bill's classmates.

Conversely, Gore and "bore" were two words that did fit together, as our "Al Gore's Diary" tried to demonstrate: "Dear Diary. Today I received my new issue of *Policy Ramifications of Third World Regulatory Policies Quarterly*. Maybe I should not admit this, but I found the section on Botswana quite provocative."

We performed for both the Clintons, along with most of official Washington, at the White House Radio & TV Correspondents Dinner in the spring of 1993, where we did a twenty-minute show. The president sat far across the enormous room, on a raised dais, looking distracted. Hillary stared humorlessly, reminiscent of Nancy Reagan. The

TRACK: 27

★★★★★★★★★★★★★★★★

The Fondler
(parody of "The Wanderer")

CLINTON
Yeah, back in Arkansas, I was the
Jock of Little Rock
The pretty girls I saw, yeah, they
Made my knees go knock
I'd ask a friendly trooper, watch the
Door and all the phones
I loved my women workers, but I
Don't love Paula Jones
She calls me the fondler
She says that I fondled her
My hands went
Around 'n 'round 'n 'round 'n 'round
'n 'round

TRACK: 28

★★★★★★★★★★★★★★★★

**Return to Center
(parody of "Return to Sender")**

CLINTON

I read a letter in the Post, an'
It said I'm way off-track
I once was lib'ral, now I'm boastin'
I'll now start movin' back

STAFF

Yeah, now he's gonna

CLINTON

Return to center
View-point unknown
No more health care
No ozone
First a flip and then a flop
There's no way I'm gonna stop
Up on Wall Street, the financiers
Always give me funny looks
Though I'll balance all the books in five

STAFF

Seven
Twelve

CLINTON

Ten years
And then I'm gonna
Move from the center
We lib'rals gonna
Have a bash
And Clinton's gonna
Return to spender
So everybody
Guard your cash

rest of the audience sat in between, in that big sunken ballroom at the Washington Hilton, looking first at us as we tried to be funny, then at the Clintons to see how (or if) they reacted. By any measure, that was the strangest show we've ever done for a president.

As we entered the 1994 election, the scandals remained petty and manageable, nothing more serious than Hillary's early friends Jim McDougal ("Old McDougal had a loan / I-O-I-O-U") and Webb Hubbell ("Hubbell / In Trouble City / With a capital T that rhymes with she / That stands for her"), and, of course, "Old Whitewater / Keep on rollin'." We were still telling the occasional Gennifer Flowers joke ("Sneakin' Flowers through the wall / That don't bother me at all"), but those were getting a little old.

That spring, Al Gore invited us to do a show at the White House (actually, the Gray House, alias the Old Executive Office Building) for his forty-eighth birthday party. Tipper would be there, we were told, along with much of the White House staff—and Big Bubba, the Prez himself would try to stop by. Recalling how we'd sanitized the post–Desert Storm show for President Bush, at the request of his staff, we didn't bother to ask Gore's staff if we should clean things up for Clinton. Per the new Nike slogan of those years, we just did it.

Sure enough, Clinton dropped by, friendly as could be. He greeted us all very graciously, let us take some photos, and then watched, laughing—of course, this was pre-Monica, and the toughest we got was "Return to Center" and "Secret Asian Man." The Gore diaries were the hit of the show, perhaps because Al was the guest of honor and his staff the audience.

That would be the last time we would perform for Clinton or Gore. Once the Paula Jones story broke, and especially after Monica, our chances to perform at the White House fell to somewhere between nil and minus infinity.

But we didn't mind. Plenty of other people were more than ready to laugh—a lot.

The '90s were roaring, and the funny business was booming. Tragedy tomorrow, comedy tonight.

10

The Great American Pleasure Palace ("Lirty Dies and Skirty Dandles")

★★★★★★★★

TRACKS: 29–31

With the arrival of these cool, stylish, and entertaining new leaders, Americans were in the mood for good times. The Capitol Steps too. We were rolling out three hundred shows a year, with two touring casts, doing hardship duty at classic resorts like the Boca Raton, at the north edge of Florida's Gold Coast. Tough life, arriving at your spa around lunch time, luxuriating at the beach until your five o'clock sound check, chasing a few sea breezes.

One bright afternoon at the Boca, Bill Strauss was about to do exactly that. On the jitney connecting the old manse with the beach house, he recognized a sixtyish man sitting directly across, who looked as though he faintly recognized Bill. The man was with his wife, lost in

TRACK: 29

★★★★★★★★★★★★★★★★★

**Fun Fun Fun 'Til Teddy
Puts His T-shirt Away
(parody of "Fun Fun Fun")**

It's the Senate spring break, and we'll
    take it with the Kennedy clan now
Clan now, Kennedy clan
Mister Teddy says he's ready, he's not
    actin' like a middle-aged man now
Man now, middle-aged man
After sunnin' watch him runnin' round the
    beach-house wearin' only a tan now
Tan now, wearin' a tan
And we'll have
Fun fun fun
Folks at home are hearing plenty
Fun fun fun
Seventeen'll get you twenty
Fun fun fun
'Til Teddy puts his T-shirt away

her own thoughts (whose relevance to our story would come much later). As everyone disembarked, that man walked up to Bill and said, "I couldn't help but wondering, do you mind if I ask you if…"

"Capitol Steps?" Bill asked.

"Yes. You guys are great."

"Are you…Senator Packwood?"

He smiled and said that he was, and he wanted to thank us for putting him in a song (about tax reform), and he was delighted, at long last, to be "in" our show.

This attitude never failed to surprise us. As a matter of fact, the only time we can remember a senator getting really mad at us was when Senator D'Amato of New York approached us after a show, complaining that we *didn't* do a song about him. "Well, get in a good scandal, and we will," was Elaina's reply, and the next thing we knew, he was the target of a grand jury investigation (unsuccessful, but it's the thought that counts).

By the time we'd been at this for ten years, we heard people tell us that getting your name mentioned in one of our songs—better still, having one of our performers play you on stage—had become a cachet separating the alphas from the betas-to-zetas in official Washington. Senators and Congressmen actually *wanted* us to make jokes about them.

That would change.

In the 1980s, the typical way a muckety-muck landed in a lyric was to introduce a major piece of legislation, like the Gramm-Rudman Deficit Reduction Act (which we skewered in our "Deficit Discounters" department store ad bit), sign a major treaty, or at the very worst get caught lying, taking petty bribes, or trading a few guns for hostages.

By the middle '90s, well, let's just say that Bob Packwood wouldn't have enjoyed seeing us play him on stage in "Can You Feel the Rub Tonight?" Or be pilloried in a routine we call, "Lirty Dies," as in, "dirty lies."

That's our tackwards balk, er a, backwards talk routine (otherwise known as spoonerisms). Becoming the subject of a "lirty dies"—as in "Wackpood, the Sex-Enator"—has become a very special résumé item

  SIXTEEN SCANDALS

in our nation's capital. It means you've made the A-list in humor, for better or (usually) worse.

"How do you ever come up with stuff like this?" People have asked us that a gazillion times after shows. And there are half a gazillion answers.

Here are some basic rules about comedy: 1) Remember the comedy "rule of three." 2) Wear a cow suit.

All right, we forgot the rule of three. Our third rule was going to be to avoid bad puns, which does not apply to cow humor. Cows have been quite in the news in recent years, from Hillary's cash cows to British mad cows. To err is human, to forgive, bovine. Brian Ash used to quip that he spent so much time on stage dressed as a cow that his autobiography should be entitled, *Once More into the Cow Suit.*

Over the years, while the nation's leaders have done quite nicely at manufacturing scandals, we've had to manufacture our responses. This definitely requires caffeine—*and* an elaborate production process, for writing parodies. When we feel the need, we search through Elaina's vast computer file of song titles looking for a good pun, write alternative drafts, settle on one, test it for laughs, and then, the audience is the judge. Do they always work? Absolutely not, although sometimes a song we weren't sure about goes gangbusters and sometimes a song we were in hysterics over backstage gets blank stares. The performer is like the canary in the coal mine sent out to test the unknown.

One of the biggest challenges, and the most fun, is writing for a specific character. Elaina's personal favorite, from a writing standpoint, was Ross Perot. What made Ross funny was that he didn't talk like a normal politician, so the writing challenge was to figure out how Ross would phrase things. For example, while a normal politician might have said, "The deficit is a serious issue," our show's Ross would say, "The deficit is like a rattlesnake in your pants. You know you have to take out your gun and shoot it, but you don't wanna hit nothin' important."

Sometimes, a song idea waits for an issue. For years, we'd wanted to do "It's My Party and I'll Cry if I Want To," but until Ross came along with his whining at the 1996 convention (and it became "It's My Party, Which I'll Buy if I Want To"), it was a song looking for a subject.

Lots of times, writing a song can be just plain hard work, with hours spent staring at a blank screen, but sometimes ideas just hit you. Like the time one of our troupes was riding a bus in Arkansas (oh, what a font of '90s humor) listening to the radio, when the song "You Can't Hide Those Lyin' Eyes" came on. Everybody sang along, until one word-smithery led to another. By the third verse, everybody was singing "you can't hide those giant thighs"—and that's how we came up with our song of that name that we first sang about dieting, later about Clinton.

Which brings us back to "Lirty Dies." In the summer of 1987, Bill was vacationing with his family, motoring through southwest Colorado. In Durango, they attended a little vaudeville revival playing in an old western-style theater where one of the bits was an old spoonerism routine by a local actor about "Prinderella and the Cince."

When Bill got home, he sent Elaina an idea for "Dicky Trick of Gaterwate," Elaina counter-proposed a current scandal, involving Senator Gary Hart—and "Lirty Dies" was born.

"Hary Gart and Ronna Dice. On the Bunkey Musiness. Where someone fook a toto. Of her litting on his sap. Then they saw the boo from the tushes."

We added bits about "Bammy Taker and her jusband, Him" and "Nollie Orth and Gontracate," put the three stories on our *Shamlet* album, and we had our first-ever *Lirty Dies*—spoony loonerisms, tubbledalking, bird watching, call it what you will, but kee bareful, or you'll thart to stink like that.

What makes Lirty Dies funny? Mangle a few complex consonants around, play with word combinations, and you can make almost any straight line sound overtly sexual, even though what you're saying is utterly G-rated.

One secret is the mother tongue, the English language. To our ear, it's the best in the world at comedy, given the potential for rhymes, puns, odd vowel and consonant sounds, you name it. We've spoken with people from France, Italy, Germany, Japan, and many other countries about this, and they agree that English gives you the most ways to make purely verbal jokes.

The other secret—well, no secret actually—is how, through the early '90s, we passed through the Great American Pleasure Palace, a nonstop string of miniscandals that kept audiences roaring and comedians in business. Mark Russell likes to call times like these "rip and read," when

all you had to do was rip out a news story, read it to the crowd, and you'd get a laugh.

None of these scandals was that huge, consequential, or long-lasting. None affected the fate of the republic. A hundred years from now, none of them is likely to be described in high school history texts. Taken together, though, they may comprise the longest string of humorously naughty celebrity/politician behavior in the history of any human society, from Caligula's Rome to Louis XVI's Paris and beyond. Or, at least, it was the longest string of salacious goings-on that a mainstream media ever *reported*.

Therein lies one key fact, underlying what was transpiring with comedy during those years. A generation earlier, as recently as the early 1970s, the press kept a more discreet distance from national leaders and other famous people. Kay Summersby, Fiddle and Faddle, Judith Exner, Marilyn Monroe, young babes at LBJ's swimming parties—these and more stayed off-limits for any journalist with a respectable career. Sure, the *Enquirer* and other rags spread gossip, but nobody paid much attention. Listen through the political satire albums of that era, and you won't find anything more than the gentlest tweak about the high-level womanizing then going on.

★★★★★★★★★★★★★★★
16 Funniest Elected Officials, U.S. History

1. Bill Clinton
2. Dan Quayle
3. Benjamin Franklin
4. Warren Harding
5. Aaron Burr
6. Richard Nixon
7. Ted Kennedy
8. Newt Gingrich
9. William Jennings Bryan
10. Daniel Webster
11. Strom Thurmond
12. Bob Packwood
13. Joseph McCarthy
14. John C. Calhoun
15. Hillary Clinton
16. John Kennedy

Those days are long gone, replaced by a new ethos that caused political comedy to burst into a new golden era. Some attribute this to Clinton, the only U.S. president ever to be funnier than a cow suit, but he was merely one of twelve steps in a national self-help plan to elevate the quantity (if not level) of comedy in politics.

Step One came when the so-called Greatest Generation won the war and celebrated by having too many babies, feeding them on demand, and raising them to be sarcastic little Lucys and Leave it to Beavers.

Step Two was when Lucy and Beaver grew up (sort of), rioted on campus, called college and national presidents terrible names—and, for punishment, received unconditional amnesties, diplomas, and jobs on Congressional staffs.

★★

Can You Feel the Rub Tonight?
(parody of "Can You Feel the Love Tonight")

WOMAN
I came up to the Congress
I found myself a job
I served a guy who comes from Oregon
A Senator named Bob
He's no worse than the next guy
Or so he liked to say
But of course the next guy is a guy named Teddy K
Can you feel the rub tonight?
Feel it on your knee
MEN
Rub-a-rub, rub-a-rub-a-rub
WOMAN
They made me read my job description
Horizontally
You'll pay for your...misconduct
PACKWOOD
Miss who?

KENNEDY
Er, a, when can we meet?
WOMAN
Election year, you watch your rear
We're gonna grab your seat
We will win election night
We'll kick you out, you louse
MEN
Rub-a-rub-a, rub-a-rub-a-rub
WOMAN
We plan to show what the woman's role is
MEN
You sure can clean the House
WOMAN
And the Senate

Step Three was Watergate. Thanks to Woodward and Bernstein's "Deep Throat," young reporters broke ground for a new national sport of investigative journalism. This was all very funny, except people didn't realize it yet. From the middle '70s through the early '80s, this new crop of reporters delved into one issue after another, generally content to be leaked stories by Nader's Raiders and others concerned with serious political issues. Toxic waste dumps? *Scandalous!* Medicaid fraud? *Scandalous!* The Pentagon spending $7,000 on a toilet seat? *Scandalous!* Risquee episodes began creeping into the discussion, involving Wilbur Mills, Wayne Hays, and Ted Kennedy (still smarting from Chappaquiddick), but remained on the periphery of real journalism.

Step Four came with cable TV. In the middle '60s, the three networks expanded news coverage from fifteen to thirty minutes. In the '70s, they added evening analysis shows like *Nightline*. Then, in the early '80s, Ted Turner gave us CNN—which, in time, proved an enormous boon for political satire. Now one heavily financed new network had twenty-four hours to devote to politics and business. By the middle '80s, investigative reporters were reaching beyond a Naderite agenda grown old, stuffy, and (worst of all) boring to the public—and were getting air time. Talking head shows felt new and fresh.

Step Five in this national comedic self-help plan arrived with the new national attitude toward sex, heralded by Surgeon General C. Everett Koop. All of a sudden, Americans were *supposed* to talk freely about sex, as a matter of life or death, not to mention proper gender relations. People of all orientations demanded an end to "closets" of all kinds.

Step Six was the late-'80s advent of conservative talk radio. Hosts like Rush Limbaugh monitored the various fringes of journalism, dispersing humorous petty tidbits to an ever-growing audience of listeners with a bottomless appetite for dirt.

Step Seven required some sucker to trip the cord and get the whole thing rolling. Enter the witless Gary Hart, who dared to deny his rumored dalliances and brazenly challenged reporters to follow him to see how nobly he lived as a loyal and monogamous family man. In the days of JFK, that challenge would have been given and received with a wink, as a coded admission made with a secret handshake. Not any more. A couple of reporters took Hart up on his challenge and trailed him to the *Monkey Business* and his Georgetown townhouse. When the story broke, the fact that Hart had issued such a foolhardy challenge persuaded serious editors that this was a bona fide news event worthy of major coverage, for a man who thought himself presidential material. Thus did the sex lives of politicians become public beyond anything ever before seen in American history.

Step Eight was the election of Clinton—a president whose humor zone matched the National League strike zone: from the belt to the upper thigh. Any President who would willingly answer questions about his underwear made himself wide open to questions about anything at all.

Step Nine was the World Wide Web, the best pure gossip machine ever invented. Scan, click, and spam. Nobody knew if down was up or I was you or boys were girls, but millions of people had loads of fun with this new toy, while leaving to others the hard questions about whether a Matt Drudge rumor might be true.

Step Ten was the arrival of a younger Generation X that could get down and dirty, in the manner of Beavis and Butt-Head, while feeling not an atom of shame.

Step Eleven was the end of the Cold War. Relieved of the only real foreign enemy of the prior forty years, Americans could go over the top—sex, violence, gross humor, anything anybody wanted—with a sense of cultural and historical invincibility.

Enter the twelfth and final step of this national self-help comedy plan. Actually, this was many steps. The Capitol Steps—and others like us. Does a tree fall if nobody's around to hear it? Is a joke funny if nobody's around to tell it?

To feed this national humor machine, we needed amusing events—and there were plenty of those in the early '90s.

The fun began with Peewee Herman ("Weepee Herman, who was copped by a stop for wickling his teeny in a florno pick"). In his mug shot, we've never seen a starker, or funnier, example of a celebrity secret unmasked.

Many Americans have a mixture of admiration, envy, and moral disrespect for TV and film stars, and when one of them gets such a huge comeuppance, it confirms our sense of comfort in not being celebrities ourselves—either because we're not going down those kinky paths, or because our own dirty little secrets never become public humiliations.

Next, we had William French Smith and "Uncle Ted" Kennedy, at a Palm Beach party that ended badly. The Kennedys are America's ersatz royalty, mixing tragedy with comedy in a stew no other family can match for sheer breadth of drama. Was it attempted rape, a clumsy advance, or a consensual if beer-sotted something else?

It pained us to think of Ted, not exactly Mister Muscle Beach, doffing his shirt around Willie's young female friends. This was great comic theater, making Ted Kennedy the only American politician whose sex-

capades spanned four decades. ("We'll have fun fun fun / 'Til our Teddy puts his T-shirt away.")

We had those sweet lovelorns, Clarence Thomas and Anita Hill. Parts of their recriminations weren't funny, but other parts definitely were. What a great mystery romance: Was she telling the truth, was he, or (more likely) was the truth somewhere in between? And what wonderful details. "Tarence Chlomas made Hanita Ill, with his song long dilver and something cubic on his poke."

Poor John Bobbitt. To have *that* happen and then be a national laughingstock? ("Borena Lobbitt thacked off his wingie and whew it in the throods, so her unspucky louse had to have sastic plurgery on his bingama thob.") We gave sweet imaginary revenge to feminists in our audience when we sent out a soprano, butcher knife in hand, singing to "Bibbiddy Bobbiddy Boo" ("Act like a chauvinist pig and you'll get / Snipped like a bobbitt in two"). Our soloists loved that song, if only to see men cross their legs and quake in their seats.

It isn't often that an event that bloody is funny, from day one, but this one most definitely was—no doubt because it rose to the level of modern myth, the reverie of many a woman and the dread of many a man.

D.C.'s own dear mayor, Marion Barry, became a comic target with his drug purchase from a prostitute, prompting us to parody "Proud Mary" as "Proud Barry." ("He lost a good job in the city / Just 'cause Mayor Barry told a little joke / He became a goner / When he said, 'Your honor / I believe that everything goes better with coke' / Showin' no repentance / Barry got himself a sentence / An' now he is goin' / Goin' / Goin' / Goin' / Goin' up the river.") When a rehabilitated Marion Barry came back to run for office, we put a joke in the show that compared him to a venereal disease. How? First, it's embarrassing. Second, it's recurring. And it responds well to drugs. Then there's the political disease that often strikes the voting public right after a popular leader gets into a scandal: *gonnareelectum.*

TRACK: 31

★★★★★★★★★★★★★★★★

Snipped Like a Bobbitt in Two (parody of "Bibbiddy Bobbiddy Boo")

I'm tired of macho talk
I'm sick of sexist carp
I've sharpened my shears
Some bulls will be steers
Once women start acting ...
Sharp
Oh, thanks to Lorena
Bobbitt we've gained a
Way to give men what they're due
Act like a chauvinist pig and you'll get
Snipped like a Bobbitt in two
Packwood and Teddy
When you're in bed, we
Don't want a roll in the hay
We'll pull up the covers and what'll
  you get?
The worm's gonna turn
You're both gonna learn
The meaning of severance pay!
Heee-yah!

Joey Buttafuoco, that blue collar villain from Long Island who talked a gullible young lover into trying to kill his wife, proved that any common man could make a national comedy show if he was a stupid enough jerk. ("Jo, Yoey, you dig bufus, you melly smechanic, jerk on my walopy!") Likewise with Tonya Harding, whose goons bashed Nancy Kerrigan's knee before the '94 Lillehammer games. ("That skigure fater hired a fig batso who stuck up with a snick, and knacked her on the whee.") "I really enjoyed playing Tanya Harding," Ann Schmitt recalls. "It was so much fun to cry in the middle of the song, and get to start over."

Michael Jackson tickled the national funnybone when he grabbed his crotch while dancing at the Super Bowl, as rumors spread of his various proclivities. ("Jikal Maxon, neither blight nor wack, is a thurgeon in his virties, who likes to crab his grotch.") How was Michael?—we would ask him in our show. "Holding my own," he'd reply.

Doctor Jocelyn Elders gave the likes of Michael and PeeWee some advice. ("Octor Delders, the quondom keen, wants to put sontra-keptivs in our kiddle lids' bunch luckets, and now she says it's KO to mank your spunkey. It only takes tun to wango.") She was very funny *and* very fired, by an Oval Office boss who had standards of decorum he was sworn to uphold.

We relished the triple scandals of Bob Packwood, Tailhook, and Army gropers at the Aberdeen Proving Ground. Each of these was highly amus-ing—unless, of course, you happened to be the female object of these tender mercies. ("Their pouths muckered, their ringers foamed, and all those limmen's wibbers were hexually sore-assed.") We honored this breed of male with a feminist anthem, "Can You Feel the Rub Tonight?" Janet Gordon recalls how she had just finished singing that song when, in mid-show, "I had a chunk of time to go to the Ladies' Room. On my way, I ran into Bob Packwood in the hallway and got the 'once over' from Mr. Packwood himself. I felt so cheap and special at the same time."

On and on went the Great American Pleasure Palace, per the new ads of those years ("Why ask why?" "Just do it." "No rules, just right"), until Jerry Springer came to one of our shows and told our cast that if we had a goat in the act he might put us on his show. We wouldn't, and he didn't.

Hey, even during these Pleasure Palace days, we tried to uphold *some* standards of decency.

  SIXTEEN SCANDALS

11

Atsa Lawyer
("What a Lie-Lie-Lie")

★★★★★★★★★
TRACKS: 32–35

If great minds think alike, so do twisted comedic minds. On the day Chief Justice Warren Burger retired, back in 1986, we sang "Bye Bye Burger." So did Mark Russell, entirely by coincidence. That happens now and then, with song parodies.

In 2001, we received a sternly worded letter from someone who claimed to have written a song parody two years earlier: "Hello Mullah, Hello Fata," to Alan Sherman's "Hello Muddah Hello Faddah" (Camp Grenada). He heard us sing a similar song, with that same cover line, on one of our 2001 radio shows, and felt that a "financial settlement" was in order. (We responded by noting that we had written the song ten years earlier, in 1991.)

The legal term for comedy, these days, is "intellectual capital," and anyone who writes or stages comedy has to be aware of the volumes of laws, cases, books, insurance rules, and miscellaneous annoyances about federal copyright law, as laid out by Congress and interpreted by the U.S. Supreme Court and the various judicial circuits.

You don't have to delve into this very far or deep before being reminded why today's Americans find lawyers so funny. Lawyers have an omnivorous gift for taking something very simple and turning it into an enormous time-, money-, and sanity-devouring mess. We've had several in our troupe (Bill, Dave Gencarelli, Dave Werner, Amy Young, Aetna Thompson-Collins). We've done dozens and dozens of shows for law firms, who have generally been good sports about laughing at their public reputation.

Through U.S. history, lawyers weren't always considered so amusing. For most of our first two centuries, we just plain didn't have that many of them. And, after World War II, when law schools began cranking them out in large numbers, lawyers were broadly perceived either as earnest champion of the public good or as people who did work so incomprehensible that nobody could make any sense of it, comic or otherwise. Listen to old LP comedy tracks from the 1950s and '60s, and apart from bits about divorces and car crashes, you won't hear much joking at their inexpense.

Come the early 1990s, however, you began seeing a surge in lawyerly novels and movies about time-clocking, neck-choking, wallet-grabbing fomenters of crime, seducers of women, and clever manipulators of public distress. Now *that's* funny. As we sang in "Atsa Lawyer," to the tune of "That's Amore": "When you see your ex-spouse / With a low form of louse / Atsa lawyer." By 1993, with two boomer lawyers as America's first family, the nation was awash with jokes about the profession.

By coincidence or not, that's right around the time lawyers, courts, and matters of copyright law became a serious matter for political parodists.

From the earliest days of the Capitol Steps, we had paid close attention to copyright law. After doing only a few shows, Elaina and Bill compiled a lyric book that we duly deposited in the Library of Congress, thereby preventing any other Congressional subcommittee from singing our lyrics. We also pored over law books and sought free advice from various friends and neighbors (when you live in D.C., around half your friends and neighbors are lawyers) to learn whether it was OK for us to borrow melodies. We got all kinds of conflicting advice, which led us to the decision many in our trade were making in the 1980s and early '90s: We decided to do it unless and until someone complained.

As recently as the 1950s, artists recorded and networks broadcast only parodies of songs that were in the "public domain"—mainly songs that predated the 1920s. Stan Freberg's lawyers warned him not to use more than three bars of any well-known song, and Tom Lehrer decided—apart from his Gilbert & Sullivan parody of "The Elements"—to avoid the legal issue entirely. In the late 1960s, Alan Sherman recorded his "My Son, the Folksinger" parodies, after which he encountered a number of legal problems. Later, Sherman had one complete album (a full parody of *My Fair Lady*, on Jewish themes) that his publisher withheld from distribution because parody rights couldn't be obtained.

In the 1970s, Mark Russell and *Saturday Night Live* began broadcasting parodies without asking permission from the song owners, relying on the doctrine of "fair use," good taste, and a prayer. Previous court cases on "fair use" were split. Judges never said as much in their opinions, but the only consistent holding seemed to be: if your parody is vulgar, you lose; and if it isn't, you win. Ours weren't, so we felt safe. The U.S. Supreme Court hadn't spoken on this parody issue for decades, though, so we couldn't be sure.

Right from the start, we preferred doing parodies over writing original melodies. A parody gives you two extra laughs per song: one at your core pun, with a line that spoofs the original and some issue of the day, and the other when you lampoon a person or issue through the prism of how the parodied song was originally performed. In "Old Man River," Old Joe sings to a river more powerful than he is, accepting fates he can't change. In a good parody of that song, a soloist sings of a powerful thing or person that can't or won't change.

These days, parodies are constantly sung on TV shows like *Saturday Night Live* and *The Simpsons*, showcased in live comedy shows like ours, and dished up at thousands of office parties. But twenty years ago, they weren't nearly as common, in part because of all the legal uncertainties.

When we recorded our first album, in 1984, we called ASCAP and BMI, offering to pay royalties for the use of melodies, and the people at the other end of the phone told us they couldn't and wouldn't accept royalties for parodies—and that we had to get permission from the owners of the song to make those recordings.

When you write parodies, asking for permission from the music industry nearly never works out. We once had an NBC-TV project fall through because network lawyers insisted we get permissions for seven songs. We did—for only one song—after three months of trying.

As we groped through the legal uncertainties, in the late '80s and early '90s, we took comfort in knowing we were well known enough around Washington, from the legal community to the Congress. We felt like pilot fish swimming among the tentacles of the sea anemones. Sure, music moguls could chomp on us if they wanted, but (we hoped) not without getting stung.

In those days, we occasionally received letters of inquiry or warning from music publishing houses. We were tempted to respond with our own version of a caustically funny letter Groucho Marx once wrote to studio lawyers over a copyright argument over *Night at the Opera*, in which he dared them to go head-to-head with him in the field of sarcasm, not law. Instead, we merely recited our position on "fair use" or (a couple of times) stopped doing the song in question.

In the early 1990s, the U.S. Supreme Court started inching its way toward us. They heard arguments in a hugely publicized case in which Jerry Falwell complained about how he'd been depicted in cartoons in Larry Flynt's *Hustler* magazine. In a decision that brought a sigh of relief to every political cartoonist in America, the Court sided unanimously with Flynt, against Falwell—as did we, in the first of several songs we've done about Falwell.

Following Operation Desert Storm, with all the parodies then hitting the airwaves, we expected we'd get our own court test soon. Right around that same time, President Bush was having difficulty filling vacancies on

  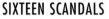

the Supreme Court. In 1990, smarting from his failure to get Robert Bork on the U.S. Supreme Court, Bush nominated an unknown judge from the woods of New Hampshire, a man with no history of opinions, viewpoints, or much of anything, beyond chopping trees for his wood stove. Nobody could dig up any dirt on the guy, so the only comedic take was to go over the top with how clean he was. That's what we did, to the tune of "If You Knew Suzy": "If you knew Souter like I knew Souter..." We accused him of knifing apple pies, ripping out mattress tags, stuff like that.

Months later, we heard that Justice Souter had heard and liked our song about him. Small wonder, given what a cream puff of a satire it was. We also heard tell that many of the Justices on the U.S. Supreme Court, including Chief Justice Rehnquist, had keen senses of humor. Which was nice to know, given that the Court itself isn't exactly a funny place.

Through American history, the Supreme Court hasn't exactly been a staple of political satire. For the first 150 years, the Court had a number of unusual, colorful justices who, from time to time, issued enormously controversial decisions, but people didn't sing funny songs or chant jokey political slogans about them. Maybe it was those black robes. It wasn't until FDR's court-packing plan, with all the talk about "those nine old men," that the justices began taking their dust-ups like everyone else.

In our early years, we tried to include Supreme Court songs when we could, even if there wasn't much texture to the humor. Then as now, most people don't know much about the justices, or about the Court itself, so our humor tended to be very basic, no edgier than having a bunch of gray-wigged guys and gals in a black-robed kick line. In the early '80s, we did a torch song featuring Justice O'Connor, who, we later learned, was a big fan of political satire.

The only Supreme Court justice who felt the sharper edge of our stick was the one with a clear comic profile: Justice Clarence Thomas.

★★★★★★★★★★★★★★★

16 Funniest Non-Elected Newsmakers, U.S. History
1. Ross Perot
2. Victoria Woodhull
3. Jesse Jackson
4. Monica Lewinsky
5. Al Capone
6. O.J. Simpson
7. Anthony Comstock
8. Benjamin Franklin
9. Linda Tripp
10. William Randolph Hearst
11. Oliver North
12. Ken Starr
13. Henry David Thoreau
14. Johnnie Cochran
15. Commodore Vanderbilt
16. Thomas Paine

★★★★★★★★★★★★★★★★

**Atsa Lawyer
(parody of "That's Amore")**

Who can blacken your eye,

Kiss your money good-bye

That's a lawyer

With the wings of a vulture to speed up
   his ambulance chase

Though he spends lots of loot

On his camel hair suit

I assure ya

Nothing looks quite as good

As a Doberman would

On a lawyer

"Terence Chlomas" and "Hanita Ill" were the stuff of a "lirty die" routine.

This was the judicial setting when, in 1993, key players in the music industry launched an attack against political song parody. As we expected, the attack came not against us, and not anywhere close to Washington, but against the parody equivalent of Larry Flynt, in a venue far less hospitable to political humor. The target was 2 Live Crew, and the locale was Music City, alias Nashville.

Having shocked Tipper Gore and other Legions of Decency with their obscene but big-selling album *Nasty as We Wanna Be*, Luther Campbell and his 2 Live Crew colleagues followed that up with a *nice*, sort of family friendly album, *Clean as We Wanna Be*. One cut on that album, "Hairy Woman," was a parody of the Roy Orbison song "O Pretty Woman," recently the title song of a Julia Roberts movie depicting an attractive white prostitute who used her profession as a path to love, marriage, and the American Dream. With parody lyrics, 2 Live Crew sang of white prostitutes with hairy legs, smelly bodies, and mean little lives.

In their lawsuit, Roy Orbison's widow and the Acuff-Rose music company did not persuade the Tennessee District Court, but did persuade two of three judges in the Sixth Circuit that this song—with black rappers asserting that white prostitutes don't look or live like Julia Roberts in the movie—was utterly devoid of political content.

It was a ridiculous, even outrageous decision. When we learned about it, we tracked down 2 Live Crew's lawyer, who said they were exhausted by the case and wanted to settle with the plaintiffs. This would have been disastrous for us, because it would have established, at least in the Sixth Circuit, that what we did was a violation of copyright law. At the time, we were doing about a dozen shows a year in that circuit, and we knew we'd be served with an unwinnable lawsuit if we didn't act.

When we offered to provide legal counsel to file a *certiorari* brief with the U.S. Supreme Court, 2 Live Crew decided to appeal. The odds against us were high: you need four Justices to grant *certiorari*, their calendar is jammed, and only about one of every fifty requests is granted. We tried something new: along with our legal brief, we submitted a fifty-minute cassette, *From Yankee Doodle to Pander Bear*, in which we spelled out the importance of political parody to America's history by singing several of the best known parodies. "Yankee Doodle." "The Star Spangled Banner." "America 'Tis of Thee." "The Battle Hymn of the Republic." We also sang parodies that chided presidents, centered political campaigns, and challenged adversaries in war.

Our cassette, we were later told, became a hot item in the back corridors of the Supreme Court. And, good news, the case was granted a hearing.

The pending case of *Acuff-Rose v. Campbell* quickly became, for parodists, the equivalent of what the *Falwell v. Flynt* case had been for cartoonists. Our crafty and brilliant attorney Bill Lane (*that's* a lawyer) joined the ACLU in writing the briefs for oral argument, and both sides got busy lining up celebrity amicus briefs. Mark Russell, Dr. Demento, and *Saturday Night Live* were on our side. Michael Jackson, Dolly Parton, and "Weird Al" Yankovich were against us.

The court held a one-hour oral argument on a cold December day. By 7:00 AM, a huge line snaked down the steps of the Supreme Court building, full of freezing people (including some of us) seeking scarce gallery seats. Luther Campbell arrived, by stretch limo, wearing a big fluffy fur coat, and was instantly surrounded by reporters from all the networks.

During the argument, per the usual plan, the justices gave slim indication of how they were leaning—and Clarence Thomas gave slim indication of whether he was awake. While they deliberated, through the spring of 1995, we truly did not know whether we would soon be out of business.

In due course, in late spring, we got the news: We won, as the political cartoonists had, by a unanimous vote. Justice Souter wrote the opinion. ("If you knew Souter / Like we know Souter / Oh, oh,

TRACK: 34

★★★★★★★★★★★★★★★

Johnnie Cochran's Fairy Tales

COCHRAN

"Little Red Riding Hood" by Johnnie Cochran.

Now, little red riding hood is the case of a wrongly accused wolf. I mean, are we supposed to believe that a wolf could actually have made it through the woods and to the grandmother's house before little red riding hood? That time line does not fit. And are we supposed to believe that a little girl's bonnet would actually *fit* this wolf? And that this little bonnet could actually convince anyone that this wolf, who lives in a human dominated society, was actually an elderly white woman? Ladies and gentlemen, this is an innocent wolf. And remember, if the face has fur, you must concur.

TRACK: 35

★★★★★★★★★★★★★★★

What a Lie-Lie-Lie
(parody of "The Boxer")

COCHRAN
Well, hello there, Mister Fuhrman
Take the oath and tell us please
Tell the truth to Johnnie Cochran
Did you find the glove of O.J.?
Does it fit him, hey, ain't no way
And the jury should hear that
Back before you joined the cops we'd like
  to know where you were at
Did you join the klan and wear a pointy
  hat?
FUHRMAN
Lie lie-lie
Lie lie-lie-lie-lie lie-lie
Lie lie-lie
Lie lie-lie-lie, lie lie-lie
Lie-lie-lie-lie, lie
I'm just a straight impartial guy
COCHRAN
What a lie lie lie

oh what a guy!") Sure, we're biased—but we think his opinion is a leading example of a judge writing clearly and wisely, in language non-lawyers can understand, on a topic of broad interest. Basically, he said it's OK for 2 Live Crew—and Mark Russell, the Capitol Steps, and so many others—to borrow melodies to poke fun at political and social issues, in live shows and on albums. (We wonder if they would have ruled this way, if they'd known that several years later we'd be singing "How Do You Solve a Problem Like Scalia?")

While this *Acuff-Rose v. Campbell* case worked its way through the court system, we had another legal case on our mind.

O.J.

Normally, homicide cases aren't the grist of comedy—especially while they're pending. Two people, wife Nicole and the luckless Ron, were cruelly murdered. (Punch line, please?) We held off, for quite awhile, as the story developed. By the time the case came to trial, though, the personalities and other oddities had turned it into enough of a freak show that our audiences were more than ready to laugh.

Mostly, we did what we usually do with wars in which people are getting killed: avoid the main event, and joke about the side shows. We sang a love song about Kato Kaelin, set to "I Left My Heart in San Francisco" ("He frosts his hair / And skims the pool / He's so cool"), an ode to Rosa Lopez (Did she or didn't she understand English?), "Won't You Go Home, Lee Bailey," a parody of "The Boxer" (with its "lie-lie-lie" riff) about Mark Fuhrman, and a take-off on "The House that Jack Built," in which we gave a soup-to-nuts account of the trial, featuring the news of any given week.

As the trial stretched on and on, nearly everybody outside the courtroom was yukking it up—but not the poor jury, sequestered from life and laughter.

Capitol Steps to the rescue!

In the spring of 1985, we had a string of shows coming up in the L.A. area, so we wrote Judge Ito, offering ourselves as jury entertainment. To our delight, the judge wrote back with an invitation. When we arrived, a marshal escorted us into a courtroom, where the jury filed in and sat in the jury box, along with two guards. "It was creepy, almost surreal, hard to describe," Brian Ash recalls. "These were arguably the most famous people in the U.S. at the time, and no one knew who they were!"

We performed for a little under an hour. Had we been in a mischievous mood, or looking to get tons of national publicity, we could have stopped the trial right then, slipping in a quick bloody glove joke before the guards could figure out what was going on. But no, we were compliant and made no jokes about the trial during our show. However, we did give each juror a set of CDs, including our songs about Kato Kaelin, Rosa Lopez, and F. Lee Bailey, along with our bit "This Is the House O.J. Built," which ended with these prophetic lines: "Here is the prison / Where his future isn' / O.J. will get zero / 'Cuz he was a hero / Who carried a ball / Each September through fall / Entertaining the twit / Who will vote to acquit."

Which, of course, they did.

"*Mistrial!*" we can hear readers screaming. Sorry, it's too late for that, because everybody's gone—to talk shows—except O.J., who's searching for the real killer between the ninth hole and the tenth tee.

Yes, the American judicial system contributed mightily to the floodtide of 1990s humor. Eventually, though, lawyers like Ken Starr and Alan Dershowitz would extend the comedic cornucopia through an even more historic trial. Once that one came and went, though, lawyer jokes were past their peak. The TV show *Survivor* recently sent a lawyer to a deserted island, prompting this question: If we can send one lawyer there, why not all of them?

Lately, we've been getting the message from people in our audiences, a great many of whom are lawyers, have children who are lawyers, or named their cats and dogs after lawyers: Back off on the L-word jokes, please—unless, of course, they're about sex or Republicans, because those topics are *always* funny.

12

A Whole Newt World
("The Right Wing's Striking Again")

★★★★★★★★★
TRACKS: 36–39

In the middle '90s, NASA sent a space probe to Mars, where it discovered something that astronomers defined, generously, as "life." This prompted our song "My Fungus Valentine," in which we explored the sweetly simple realm of unicellular sex, sung by the fictitious earthbound girlfriend of the Mars life-form. ("He left me to go to Mars four and a half billion years ago, saying he needed 'space.' When I found him, he was totally into rock.")

Speaking of prehistoric life forms, the Rolling Stones were back on tour. Most of their fans were baby boomers who, turning fifty, while busily exploring the sweetly simple realm of unicellular phones, still believed themselves totally into rock. ("Angie" became

TRACK: 36

★★★★★★★★★★★★★★★★

The Loonies of the Right
(parody of "Phantom of the Opera"
and "Music of the Night")

DEMOCRAT
What is the matter, please
With Speaker Newt?
Compared to Clinton, he's
Not half as cute
Go tell the Speaker he
Should watch his tongue
And never tell the voters that he might
Just eat their young
NEWT
Limbaugh hugs me
I'm not such a meanie
Clinton bugs me
He calls me a weenie
Congress now belongs to me
And I rule the G.O.P.
Since my party made me Speaker, now
  we might
Give power to the loonies of the right

"Angie-oplasty"…followed by "I see a bald spot, and I want it painted black"…"You can't always eat what you want / but if you're smart instead / you'll bake some bread / and eat what you knead"…and from *Rubber Soul* to rubber pants, "We'll get by with a little help from Depends.")

Meanwhile, boomers were mostly voting Republican.

Why? You had to be there, and be one, to understand. Back in the '60s, they were thrown out by their deans for getting whacked out on weed. Now, in the '90s, they were deans throwing their backs out from weed whackers.

Boomer men had become Little League screamers and Limbaugh dittoheads, having long ago turned the dial from chimeric pop stations to choleric talk radio. Boomer women had become soccer moms and devotees of Dr. Laura, into NPR and gourmet radio. The Righties bought SUVs in olive drab, distancing themselves from the Lefties, who also bought SUVs, but painted eco-green, much like boomer Bill Gates built an enormous mansion with a twenty-car garage which the media somehow declared "environmentally friendly."

"You say you want a revolution / Well, you know," sang the Beatles a quarter century earlier. Wouldn't you know it: the first true revolution the boomers ever achieved on their own was the Republican Revolution of 1994. Point of fact, this was the biggest generational landslide in over a century, and the conservative fortysomethings flocking to Congress, and to state houses around the U.S., were bold, ideological, determined, ambitious, driven to implement their moral agenda, but if you had to pick a single word to describe them, it would have to be: *funny*.

Take Newt Gingrich. (Please.)

Actually, we *were* pleased. As third in the line of succession, House speakers should carry their fair share of the comedic load. Run down the list of speakers of our lifetime, and the trend is clear. Sam Rayburn, John McCormack, and Carl Albert were not funny men. Tip O'Neill was, sort of, with his burly manner and puffy face, but he was the kind of guy you'd toast and share a Coke with, not roast and make a joke of. Jim Wright? He was goaded out by an upstart named Newt Gingrich because Jim got in trouble, yes, but unlike other Democrats, he got in trouble *with* his (on-his-payroll) wife—a big offense at the time, trivial these days. Tom Foley got beaten in the '94 Republican landslide, a fate unthinkable for a speaker. ("Hang down your head, Tom Foley / Hang down your head and cry / Go back to bed, Tom Foley / You had to go bye-bye.") Then came Newt.

Everything about the man was laugh bait, from his unscripted style to the way he carried himself, to what he did, to who his supporters were, to the tub of trouble he always seemed to land in, head first. Through his five-year tenure, he always seemed to play Wile E. Coyote to Bill Clinton's Roadrunner, getting smashed by an Acme safe while Clinton ran through a tunnel door painted on some canyon wall. Think about it…Bill Clinton has sex with an intern, and it's eventually *Newt* who has to resign as a result.

Block Clinton's budget? Sure, Newt. Clinton shuts down Yellowstone and Yosemite, and it's *your* fault. ("I can show you my world / Whining, bickering gridlock… / A whole Newt world / A pre-Jurassic point of view.")

Cut funding for dirty art? Sure, Newt. Clinton weeps over some minor cuts for some widows and orphans program, and it's *your* fault. (Newt was perfect as the Grinch in "How the Ging-Grinch Stole Congress.")

Speak up against Clinton's policy on Israel? Sure, Newt. Clinton invites you on Air Force One but makes you leave ingloriously by the back door, and the press depicts *you* as the crybaby. ("It's Newt, Newt, Newt goin' out my back door.")

Release the Starr Report, savaging Clinton's lies and infidelities and the nation's loss of moral compass? Sure, Newt. Meanwhile, you're sneaking around with your own cutie. ("A whole Newt world / A world of many Newtered things / We're Newtralizing everything but Newt.")

Through the '90s, we sang one parody—"The Loonies of the Right"—with a shifting set of characters—Jerry Falwell, Bob Dole, Rush Limbaugh, but it landed best with, and on, poor Newt.

TRACK: 37

★★★★★★★★★★★★★★★

**The Right Wing's Striking Again
(parody of
"Lightning's Striking Again")**

BUCHANAN
Did you lose your jobs to Europe or
Japan?
Ooo-wah-ooo
You blue-collar slobs could use a Genghis
Khan
Ooo-wah-ooo
Tell the liberal nuts, in their cotton Docker
clothes
Ooo-wah-ooo
We will cane their butts, and we'll hang
them by their toes
Watch this old talk-show host
Give a Rush to the dittoheads
Left-wing pinkos are toast
I will crush what they do in bed
Let me offer my pledge
To go off the deep edge
Stop
I can't stop
Stop
I can't stop
The right wing's striking agai-ain
Right wing's striking again and again,
we are angry white men

("Limbaugh hugs me / I'm not such a meany / Clinton bugs me / He calls me a weenie / And I rule the G.O.P. / Since my party made me speaker, now we might / Give power to the loonies of the right.")

When Newt abandoned his position, at the height of the Clinton impeachment saga, the Republicans briefly managed to find precisely the one member of the House whose own member problem may have been worse than Clinton's: Bob Livingston. His brief cascade from power confirmed that Republican politicians can't even talk about these matters like most people. It was never sex or an affair, just a series of youthful indiscretions, and he's gone anyway, so why keep talking about it?

Sex is always funny, but for Republicans, illicit sex in small doses can be oddly humanizing. The mostly Democratic mainline media agonized over whether to report George Bush's rumored weekend tryst, while vice president, with a diplomat his own age—or an adulterous affair Bob Dole had nearly three decades before—and eventually decided against reporting any of it. Could it be for fear that spreading rumors like those would have *gained* votes for a Republican?

The G.O.P. eventually turned to a wrestling coach from the heartland, Dennis Hastert, who by all accounts may be the least likely denizen of the House to score young interns, no matter how power-struck they might be. If their goal was to slow the gears of the humor machine—well, they got their wish.

Republicans tend to be more white, male, and affluent than Democrats, making them easier to barb. Democrats, meanwhile, have succeeded nicely in protecting some of their goofier edges from comedy by establishing the theology that you must be very careful when joking about nonwhites, females, and the poor, unless you personally inhabit one (or, better, all three) of those categories yourself.

Also, while Democrats go for lunch-bucket, senior's, and children's issues, worthwhile or not, the G.O.P. tends to jump on issues that seem more peripheral to the average Jane and Joe's workaday life. "Cut taxes" is one mantra, but when the words "for the rich" are added to that sound bite, it packs a different punch.

As a special comedic bonus, there were all those garden variety right-wing nut-case extremists—who, unlike garden variety left-wing nut-case extremists, we could cook to burnt toast with zero risk of getting in media trouble. ("I can't stop / I can't stop / The right wing's striking again and again and again and again.") From Waco to Ruby Ridge, we had loads of fun with the "black helicopter" crowd ("Glory, glory paranoia") and the Attorney General they hated so ("She's the middle-aged lady named Janet Reno").

"Wondering why Republicans are funny is kind of like asking why the French are funny," says Eaton, who has played both in our show. "Everyone just accepts it."

The Capitol Steps have accepted it too, despite our own Republican origins—or, perhaps, *because* of that. Not many humorists bear to other than the port side, and once we developed a reputation for playing it fair, we began to get bookings from business groups, trade associations, wealthy individuals throwing lavish parties for a few thousand of their closest friends, those kinds of things.

Even our most liberal Democratic cast members, and there are several, came to enjoy a Republican-style life on the road, entertaining Republicans in swank resorts, wallets bulging with premier executive gold platinum airline cards. Democratic audiences were usually noisier, but after the show we'd retire to a Motel 6 down by the strip mall. The worse the hotel, the better the audience. Maybe that's how the gods of politics even things out.

Take note of the political satirist's leisurely lifestyle: up at 5:00, to the

★★★★★★★★★★★★★★★★
16 Nations with the Most Punchlines
1. USA
2. Iraq
3. France
4. Israel/Palestine
5. Afghanistan
6. Outer Space
7. Russia
8. Yugoslavia
9. China
10. United Kingdom
11. Panama
12. India
13. Nicaragua/El Salvador
14. Libya
15. Canada
16. Germany

airport at 7:00, off at 8:00, land at 11:00, get where you're going by 1:00, have lunch, do a sound check at 5:00, dinner at 7:00, show at 9:00, clap clap clap cheer cheer cheer, back to your room at 11:00, try to sleep, wake up call at 6:00, to the airport at 7:00, repeat the above.

Honolulu is Hoboken when viewed this way.

Little mistakes could and did happen. Airlines sometimes lost our prop bags. If you're a shopkeeper in Somewhere, USA, and once had a customer asking for a Clinton wig and Monica beret, it was probably us, desperate to assemble a few essentials on the late afternoon before a sold-out evening show.

The show must go on, and nearly always did. Only three times, out of six thousand shows, have we failed to live up to that motto. Our alibis: we were rioted out in L.A., after the Rodney King verdict was announced. We were flooded out in Baltimore, where Amtrak was Sidetrak for seven hours, thanks to rising waters. And we were ratted out at Stanford, where rodents chewed through some wires and cut off all the campus's electrical power.

Yes, the G.O.P.-led mid-1990s was a golden era of comedy-on-the-go, during which there was indeed no business like the comedy show-on-the-go business. By the middle '90s, we had expanded to two, three, and then four troupes, all of which could be on the road at the same time. We once had two casts fly from D.C. to Palm Springs in the same plane, and two casts who performed in the same Manhattan hotel, separated by one thin wall.

The election year of 1996 may have been more interesting for satire than politics. The return of Clinton-Gore looked like a gimme, despite Hillary's revelation that she was channeling with Eleanor Roosevelt and Gandhi, which gave us an excellent chance to reintroduce cow jokes into our show. ("The Gandhi man tells you / Never have a cow / Because your caste is so good.") The economy was robust, and Republican candidates limped through the primary with precious few issues, other than Jack Kemp's quarterback tax cut. ("Pay your tax, get a quarter back.")

Bob Dole won the nomination, less on charm than résumé. Dole's personality brought to mind Ronald Reagan getting up on the wrong side of the bed (if Reagan ever got out of bed). Where the Gipper had seemed quite in joint for the early 1980s, Dole was clearly out of it by the middle 1990s.

It wasn't Morning in America any more, and this World War II–winning generation felt like a spent force in politics, having been on major party presidential tickets dating back to Tom Dewey in 1944. The boomer-led Culture War was in full flower, Gen X was roaring with new technologies, schoolkids were the top national priority, and voters didn't want old poppa running the show any more.

This mismatch between the man and the moment is what made Bob Dole so funny. To portray him, we recycled the Reagan wig, stuck the mike in the right hand, gave a scowl, and blurted out lines like mortar rounds. Dole was the first American politician we could make funny by making him seem mean. Not Gingrichy mean, but *real* mean, as in our song "It's Not Easy Bein' Mean."

One of his oddities was his curious way of never referring to himself in the first person. Many politicians say the royal "we" instead of "I," but Dole took that kingly act one step further by constantly using his own name as a pronoun. This produced an effect that surely would have made him wince, had he ever seen us do it. "Yes, Bob Dole lost the election. And Bob Dole also lost the ability to refer to Bob Dole in the first person....This dates back to Bob Dole's wedding day, when Bob Dole told Liddy Dole, 'Bob Dole do,' and Bob Dole gave Liddy Dole a diamond that was so small, it was nearly invisible to the naked Bob Dole."

For awhile, Bob Dole was so funny, some of us who disagreed with his politics were actually hoping he'd beat Bill Clinton. (This, of course, was pre-Monica, and none of us would be saying that a year later.)

Where Carter, Mondale, Dukakis, and Bush had faded from the comic radar within weeks after losing a presidential election, Dole stayed there by getting a face lift and doing ads for Viagra.

Oddly, Dole himself didn't see the humor in this. At one event where the defeated G.O.P. candidate was the honored guest, Brad Van Grack walked over to him and asked if we could do the Viagra song. Without

★★★★★★★★★★★★★★★★

**Viagra
(parody of "Maria")**

BOB
What's the most beautiful thing Bob Dole ever buys?
LIDDY
Viagra, Viagra, Viagra, Viagra
BOB
What can help Bob Dole make Bob Dole's poll now rise?
LIDDY
Viagra, Viagra, Viagra, Viagra
BOB
Viagra, thank god for
Viagra
Bob Dole met a pill named Viagra
Bob Dole will never stop
Bob Dole is back on top, again
Viagra

looking up, Dole shot back, "You do that song, and I am leaving."

It's not easy being mean.

Bob Dole wasn't the only Washingtonian to feel a sense of siege after the '96 election. By then, a lot of jokes were beginning to rub raw, even as we were unwittingly hurtling toward comedic events that would soon displace the eye of Newt or the dilemma of Dole as the vortex of all jokes.

On election day, 1996, Bill Strauss was on an airplane returning home from a show, when he recognized former Senator George McGovern sitting across the aisle. McGovern was Dole's age and generation, also a decorated war veteran who had tried but failed to be president. He and Bill had crossed paths a quarter century earlier, in the Senator's heyday. Bill said hello, and the two of them talked. The subject quickly turned to Clinton's prospects. McGovern seemed surprisingly downcast about the likelihood that the president would win. Recalling Nixon's Watergate scandal that had erupted within months after drubbing his own candidacy, forty-nine states to one, McGovern warned Bill that, soon after Clinton's reelection, there would probably be some huge new scandal that would come out of nowhere and ruin his second term.

Across the aisle, Bill was smiling.

13

The Full Monica
("Unzippin' My Doodah")

★★★★★★★★★
TRACKS: 40–42

In December 2001, while promoting an HBO special featuring her continuing quest to redeem some privacy in a wicked world where her last name had become both noun and verb, Monica Lewinsky urged America's comedians to limit themselves to jokes that were "pleasant."

Well, in 1997—the year she and Bubba were secretly forging the raw ingot of ten million jokes—we were indeed awash in "pleasant" humor, whether we liked it or not. By the standards of that raucous decade, that year's scandals were mild, involving money more than sex.

Clinton and Gore were settling in for a second term, and anyone with enough money settled into the Lincoln bedroom for the night,

TRACK: 40

★★★★★★★★★★★★★★★

**Unzippin' My Doodah
(parody of "Zippideedoodah")**

CLINTON
In my oval office study
It's the truth
It's factual
Everything is satisfactual
I'm unzippin' my doodah
Every day
Some cute intern could be headed
    my way
Plenty of fun times
People to meet
No, it's not cheatin'
If I'm on my feet
Close the door and lock the deadbolt
Cause I got a new date
Chelsea has a brand new roommate
So, I'll zip up my doo-dah, I'm not a slob
Hey I'm the boss man
Can I keep this job?

only a hundred thousand dollars a pop. (Possible amenities? Complimentary Bob Packwood hand lotion and a Ted Kennedy–sized minibar?) We imagined corporate contributions enticing Clinton to change the name to the Lincoln Continental Bedroom.

Al Gore's fund-raising efforts were by now global and legendary, involving Taiwanese merchants, Indonesian go-betweens, and Buddhist Nuns ("nudist buns," in backwards talk)—quite a humorous picture, given Gore's image of stiff rectitude. We superimposed a ridiculously un-James-Bond-like Al Gore over a James Bond musical theme, showing us the money from "Secret Asian Man."

That world-class comic instigator, Paula Jones, was persisting in her lawsuit. The question of whether Paula Jones could sue a sitting president raised thorny questions. Could Paula ask to see the president's briefs? And what if the jury was…well…hung? By 1997, though, we'd reached the point where Paula jokes were getting a little tired from overuse.

The closest comedians could get to anything fresh, raw, and steamy was across the Potomac, where NBA broadcaster Marv Albert stood trial for allegedly having bitten a woman's back in a moment of passion. This offered perhaps our most notable success at using computer rhyming dictionaries, when Elaina ran "chew" into a sound-alike program and came up with "Pardon Me Miss, Is this the Chap Who Tried to Chew You." Through the year, "marmy Smarv" gave us our best new lirty die ("the cort-spaster found a dabulous fish, unbluttoned her bouse, and tit her borso."), and we were still doing "Mick Dorris" ("who got hot with a cooker, tucking her soze and ficking her leet"), another top staffer fired by Clinton for not being a "sponogamous mouse," not "upholding the American lay of wife."

The Culture War was still manufacturing jokes, left and right. As usual, we went after both sides. In a comic windfall, the Southern Baptist convention summoned its members to boycott those devil-worshipers at Disney. Maybe they were onto something: if you rearranged the letters in Michael Eisner's last name, and added an I and a U and an F, you got: *Lucifer*. Small wonder Goofy and Mickey were domestic partners, and Beauty a little too enthralled with that bestiality thing. Unctuous sanctimony is always funny. Mike Tilford brought out his best Southern Baptist preacher for our show-opening "I *have been* to the mountain! *Splash* mountain!"

Israel was still arguing with Arafat ("Hava No Deala"), but otherwise nearly nothing was happening overseas, amusing or otherwise, but up in space the MIR space station was eminently funny because it fed into our preconceived notions of Russians in run-down living spaces with a shortage of amenities, ergo our fictitious Russian TV show, "This Old MIR."

The new national villain was Bill Gates, who pretty much ran the country, and the new national tragedy was a shortage of Beanie Babies. In a move that may have been ahead of its time—our pianist Lenny Williams called us "the Coltrane of comedy" (or did he mean "coal train"?)—we took on corporate America. We gibed telemarketers, per *Bali H'ai*, in "MCI is calling." And, thanks to a national outbreak of e-coli, we could yet again order our cast into cow suits to parody "My Melancholy Baby" by crooning "my swell e-coli baby," and three cows flapping hooves in our "YMCA" parody, "USDA."

In 1997, America's corporate culture was booming, and Americans by the millions were trying to cash in on the stock market, but the topical comedy industry faced a bit of a recession. Audiences felt soft, the jokes recycled. Nothing much new was happening in the culture. Bookings fell. The pop music business was also struggling with falling CD sales and a new sense of staleness.

That also happened to be the year we opened Off-Broadway for the first time, in the John Houseman Theater on 42nd Street. It turned out not to be the best moment for fresh-from-the-news crackling-hot political satire. The Manhattan economy was booming, the crime rate was plunging, Rudy Giuliani was in Phase One of being fitted for a halo, Clinton sex jokes were at least two years passe, so while the locals on the whole liked our style of humor, some of the sharper pens found it a little, well...*pleasant*.

Yes, as 1997 ended, we needed a little bite in our show.

Enter Monica.

We got wind of her the way many Americans were starting to get their scandal news, on the Internet, a few days before the scandal rocked the mainstream media. We got right to work, as no doubt all America's comedians did. We had a new show opener, apologies to Handel ("Yay, a scandal / Enormous scandal / Hallelujah, hallelujah, *hall-e-lu*-jah!") along with several other hastily-written songs ("Bimbo Eruption" to "Rainbow Connection"—and, to celebrate the scandalmongers, "Take it Sleazy" to "Take it Easy").

If comedy is based on exaggeration, then this new scandal presented a special challenge for comedians. How do you exaggerate events already so ridiculous they were almost unbelievable?

A phone rings, and the president picks it up and says, "Hello, Clinton here. Well, hi there. What's wrong? Hey, listen, I don't care about the subpoena, there's no way anyone's gonna be able to prove that you and I had a sexual relationship. Just calm down, Hillary. Hello? Hello?"

America wanted The Full Monica, and we gave it to 'em. Within two weeks after the scandal broke, we'd added two songs that would become Steps classics—"Unzippin' My Doodah" ("Plenty of fun times, people to meet / And hey, it's not cheatin', if I'm on my feet") and "Old Man Zipper" ("We gave Bill Clinton a test on morals / He passed the written / But flunked his orals"), in which we revealed the only babe in Washington Clinton hadn't hit on: Janet Reno.

Clinton's penchant for diversion prompted our Abbott and Costello take-off, "Who Hired Her First," in which an exasperated reporter grilled the elusive Clinton. ("Did anybody see the two of you alone together?" / "Not anybody. Nobody saw us." / "Do you have intimate knowledge about anything?" / "Look, if you guys in the press knew anything, you'd figure it out." / "Have you ever been on top of anything?" / "Ooooh, yeah!")

We had perhaps our best ever lirty dies, "Imbos in the Boffice," featuring "Wick Slillie" and, by now, the long litany of Flennifer Jowers ("with her burvaceous cody and barge lust"), Jaula Pones ("she saw his

SIXTEEN SCANDALS

mistinguishing dark"), Wathleen Killey ("did he beeze her squoobs? Did he put her gland on his hand?"), and "Lonica Moo-insky," yet another cow joke ("She really socked his knocks off").

Part of what made this scandal so funny was that, throughout the worst of it, the Scandalman-in-Chief didn't appear all that concerned. "I did not have sex with that woman—Monica Lewinsky." He still seemed to be that Georgetown frat boy roaming for dates. By midsummer, that "Unzippin' My Doo-Dah" song—which became the title of our 1998 album and off-Broadway show—exactly expressed his jaunty attitude.

★★★★★★★★★★★★★★★
16 States with the Funniest Politicians

1. Texas
2. Florida
3. Massachusetts
4. New York
5. Indiana
6. Arkansas
7. Tennessee
8. Kansas
9. District of Columbia
10. Vermont
11. Minnesota
12. California
13. Missouri
14. Utah
15. Colorado
16. Illinois

What an embarrassment of riches. Monica was so funny for so many reasons. We depicted her in a blue dress and blue beret, a Dan Quayle intellect gone Valley Girl clueless and Madonna naughty, a woman scorned who "was so mad, she had half a mind…" What was that she was wearing? A thong? This was not a woman who should have been wearing a thong. Was it by Lane Byrant? She kept the dress? Who keeps a stained dress? Well, *we* did too, for our song "Our Love is Here to Stain," in which Clinton tried to apply a little spray stain-remover while distracting Monica with sweet talk.

You could not have made this stuff up. We won't even bring up the cigar, except it appears we just did. ("It's a wrong waste of Tiparillos….")

And Linda Tripp? We put her in a hideous wig, big baggy dress, serenaded by a torch singer ("She gets real nasty with people she likes / Each day for breakfast, she eats nails and spikes / She wires her body with cords and with mikes / That's why that Linda is a Tripp"). Our punch line—"We know why Linda's vindictive and mad / She has uncovered more sex than she's had"—was as tough as anything we ever laid on Clinton. And, of course, in lirty dies, we described her as "utt bugly. On a scale of ton to when, she is a ton. With a bape deck in her tubes."

★★★★★★★★★★★★★★★★

**Livin' Libido Loco
(parody of "La Vida Loca")**

CLINTON
She's in a great position
With fat cats and liberal dolls
I've got a premonition
My wife's gonna win this fall
I feel the urge to cheat now
My wife's gone, I'm in the clear
She'll chase a Senate seat now
I'll chase a seat right here
INTERN
Bill, can we take our clothes off
And go dancin' in the rain?
CLINTON
Don't get me cheatin' on my wife
I'm gonna feel her pain
She is drivin' me insane
While the wife is out
Livin' libido loco
Interns sure put out
Clinton's libido loco
Though it would be wrong
While Hillary's a New Yorker
Let's go flash a thong
With Clinton's libido's loco
C'mon
Livin' libido loco
C'mon
Lovin libido loco

The president picks up a phone and says, "Hi, can you get me Charlton Heston?... Hey, Charl, it's Bill. Listen, you played Moses, right?...So, you know that controversy over whether or not schools should be allowed to post the nine commandments?...You're kidding...I thought that one was demoted to 'youthful indiscretion.'...Hello? Hello?"

Sure, there was the occasional diversion from other news—Saddam acting up every now and then, Oprah mentioning she didn't like beef, causing sales to drop dramatically (and putting us back in those cow suits), and El Niño changing the weather. Those days, you could blame Clinton for everything, even El Niño, because he was busily digging himself in ever deeper and deeper, with his famous quote about what the meaning of "is" is. ("You say 'is' is is / I say 'is' isn't / Let's call the whole thing off.")

Although Hillary refused to dump the guy—what comedy that would have made—we got huge laughs by recycling our old "cut like a Bobbitt in two," with Hillary wielding the butcher knife. Later, we added a song about Buddy the Dog, the only thing in the White House that was getting fixed.

The scandal fever took new directions in August, when Clinton finally gave that long-sought, long-fought grand jury testimony that later led to the perjury count for impeachment. All of a sudden, Clinton's behavior turned surly, and the very fact of the scandal became a little less funny and more contentious.

Soon thereafter, Special Prosecutor Ken Starr released his voluminous report applying his years of education, experience, and expertise to providing incontrovertible proof that oral sex was indeed sex—and, just as Ken was getting down and dirty at the Government Printing Office, we began getting feedback

from adults in our audiences to please, keep it clean. As entertainers who'd built a corporate market, we also had to be concerned about meeting planners, often claiming to be speaking for uptight CEOs and their prim spouses. Our challenge was to be cleaner than the nightly news.

For years, America had been neatly divided into two camps: Clinton lovers and Clinton loathers. Now, as the House impeachment debate wore on, and the Senate trial loomed, each of those two camps divided into two camplets: those who wanted to keep hearing Clinton jokes, and those who didn't.

Among Clinton lovers, there were those who simply found the man (and the scandal) jolly good fun—but others who felt the humor was feeding into the "vast right-wing conspiracy" first to destroy him, and then to replace him with a Genghis Khan Culture War conservative, a switch from oral sex to Oral Roberts.

Among Clinton loathers, there were those who enjoyed wallowing in the man's humiliation, and so much the better if it destroyed him in the end—but others who just couldn't take one more crotch joke.

Those of us who were profiting so merrily and unendingly from it all were definitely with the pro-joke camplets on both sides, but every now and then we'd get that request: "Can you do a topical show with no Clinton sex jokes?" Sure. How about a Kentucky Derby with no horses?

Through it all, we did our best to keep our show PG-rated, but here were the likes of Peter Jennings and Ken Starr using words and naming body parts that we had never used, even in a comedy show. For Peter, that may have been in character, but for Ken? A man who actually answered the "never ask anybody that" question about whether he'd ever cheated on his spouse? On the one hand, it was funny to have a sly cheater like Newt Gingrich brimming with moral outrage over Clinton. Yet, on the other, it was just as funny to have clean-cut Ken, a "sponogamous mouse" in lirty talk, going after him at the same time.

We did a show at the Starr house, shortly after Ken had announced his retirement from the case. It was a Christmas party, to which he and his wife Alice had invited all the assistant special prosecutors. As you can imagine, we were on our best behavior. Our hosts cleared out a little area in front of the living room Christmas tree, and we proceeded to perform all our Grade-A Clinton material, along with bits poking fun at Clinton's various inquisitors and detractors. Bill sang our Ken Starr number ("When you're fishing like Ken Starr / Makes no difference who you are / In your bedroom I'll be playing peekaboo"), wearing our custom Ken Starr hairpiece, also known as our Al D'Amato and Alan Greenspan hairpiece, a half-bald wig with a few long gray combover locks. After the song, which the Starrs and staff thoroughly enjoyed, Ken took the wig, put it on, and never looked better.

That fall and winter, we were often asked to perform at little pocket gatherings of Republicans, which made us wonder: through all of this juiciest of scandals, was it possible Republicans were just a little...jealous? Was their impeachment trial merely an effort to carve out a role for themselves in all the fun stuff?

The president is in the middle of a phone call when he is interrupted:
President: *"Uh, senator, can you hold on a second? (cupping his hand over the phone) Yeah, come on in, honey, you're looking good, sweetheart, I'll be right with you, I'm trying to talk to some senator, you just stay right there...*
Senator: *Hello? Hello? Mr. President?*
President: *Ooooh, yes!*
Senator: *Mr. President, I was wondering if you might support a multimillion dollar hydroelectric dam in my state.*
President: *Damn! That's good!*
Senator: *Well, I appreciate that sir, because many of the Congressional Democrats are trying to stop it.*
President: *No! Don't stop! Just keep going...*
Senator: *Well, how much funding would you approve?*
President: *More! More!*
Senator: *Gee, thanks, Mr. President. (click)*

The autumn impeachment debate was more amusing for revelations of Republican sex than from anything Clinton had ever done. Week after week, new rumors flew—about Bob Livingston, who quickly resigned as House speaker, and about all sorts of other bigwigs, in tales told around

  SIXTEEN SCANDALS

the Internet, traceable to porn king Larry Flynt, who gleefully established himself as one of the president's most active defenders. Things were getting nasty, and the public was getting confused and upset, neither of which is good for a gag. Even a comedy troupe has to be a little careful turning wild rumors into punch lines, so we played it a little safe, sticking to tried-and-true material from the spring and summer. Out of control zippers, dirty dresses, and zealous prosecutors were still funny, thank goodness for us.

Come January 1999, the Senate impeachment trial wasn't nearly as exciting as the prior twelve months had been. Exit the combover and enter the big white wig, as we shifted the jokes from Ken Starr to Henry Hyde, but nothing particularly funny came out of the trial. By then, the scandal was a wrap, comically and otherwise. What more could anyone say? What new joke could anyone tell? When Juanita Broaddrick accused the president of a two-decade-old rape, the nation didn't pay attention, and comedians laid off. The impeachment steak was cooked, done, overdone. By February, it was at long last time, as Clinton's apologists had asserted for months, for Americans—including comics—to "get over it."

The president's accusers limped away, having failed at their main objective. Final score? Newt Gingrich: gone. Bob Livingston: gone. Ken Starr: Gone. Bill Clinton: still there. But the G.O.P. did succeed in dragging it on and on, until each time the scandal looked like it might fizzle, they found a new way to give it new life and drag it on and on again. This was an incredible gift to comedy, right up there with when Clinton's own sweet loving mama decided, what the hell, let's do it tonight and go to term with the bundle.

The Republicans succeeded at one other thing: the legacy of Clinton comedy. Many great leaders of many great nations have been flagrantly caught *in delicto*—perhaps not quite so humiliatingly, or adolescently,

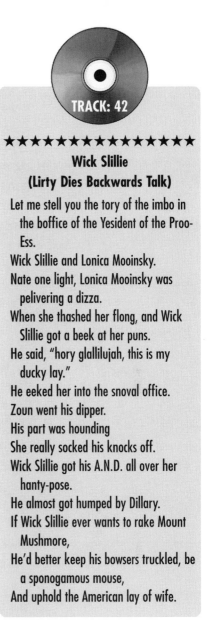

TRACK: 42

★★★★★★★★★★★★★★★
Wick Slillie
(Lirty Dies Backwards Talk)

Let me stell you the tory of the imbo in the boffice of the Yesident of the Proo-Ess.

Wick Slillie and Lonica Mooinsky.

Nate one light, Lonica Mooinsky was pelivering a dizza.

When she thashed her flong, and Wick Slillie got a beek at her puns.

He said, "hory glallilujah, this is my ducky lay."

He eeked her into the snoval office.

Zoun went his dipper.

His part was hounding

She really socked his knocks off.

Wick Slillie got his A.N.D. all over her hanty-pose.

He almost got humped by Dillary.

If Wick Slillie ever wants to rake Mount Mushmore,

He'd better keep his bowsers truckled, be a sponogamous mouse,

And uphold the American lay of wife.

with not so many details told—but jokes have their way of fading away in time. A decade later they're stale. A century later, they're barely comprehensible, as crinkly as the pages of some old book. Is Yankee Doodle's line about "Stuck a feather in his cap and called it macaroni" still funny to any living soul of the twenty-first century? Of course not.

In Clinton's case, however, history may make an exception. If so, it'll be partly from what he and Monica did, partly from what Paula Jones and Ken Starr did, but we think it will mostly be because of what Henry Hyde did—in attaching that impeachment asterisk to the Clinton legacy.

The Clinton-Lewinsky scandal is a comic gift that will keep on giving, long after our own time. We can foresee, some far off day in the 2200s, or 4400s, or 6600s, for as long as there is an America, for as long as there are history or civics textbooks, for as long as sap still flows in the human species, some schoolkid will ask "Why did Bill Clinton get impeached?," some schoolteacher will feel obliged to answer that question, and those kids will laugh and laugh and laugh.

What a pleasant thought.

14

Careful the Things You Say ("So Tell Me What You Did?")

★★★★★★★★
TRACKS: 43–44

At one of Bill Clinton's many inaugural balls, in 1993, Barbra Streisand tellingly sang a lyric from Stephen Sondheim's musical *Into the Woods*:

"Careful the things you say, children will listen / Careful the things you do, children will see."

He said; they listened. He did; they saw.

They listened and saw not just what the president did, but how special prosecutors, news reporters, talking heads, and political comedians handled it too. Blue dress? Cigar? How can you present that in a family friendly way? As Ross Perot might say, it's like two porcupines on their honeymoon. It has to be done very carefully.

TRACK: 43

★★

Unzip Unzip, Ah!
(parody of "Wannabe")

MONICA
Monica was Clinton's lover

LINDA
Linda Tripp was your friend
Now we will discover how a friendship ends

MONICA
Clinton treated me so dearly
He was once my own

LINDA
Please repeat that clearly in my microphone
So tell me what you did, what you really really did

MONICA
I'll tell you what we did, what we really really did

LINDA
So tell me what you did, what you really really did

MONICA
I'll tell you what we did, what we really really did
He went an'

LINDA
Huh?

MONICA
He went an'

LINDA
Huh?

MONICA
He went an'

LINDA
Huh?

MONICA
He went an'

LINDA
Huh?

MONICA
He went an'

LINDA
Huh?

MONICA
He went an' really really really went unzip-unzip, ah!

Through the 1980s, except for Gary Hart's adventure on the *Monkey Business*, this was not a problem—much to our consternation. Recalling all the sex scandals of the late '70s, and the Jenrette flap that gave us our name, we expected political moguls to offer up a steamy side of the Reagan years. It didn't happen. Our show had to follow the news, and the news was decidedly nonsexual.

In the 1990s, though, sex topped the news week after month after year. This served up delicious opportunities, especially for stand-up comics in adult settings. Yet it posed a pernicious challenge for those like us, who made a habit (and maybe even took pride) in presenting an act the whole family could enjoy.

The satirists of our own youth—quipsters like Tom Lehrer, Stan Freberg, and Alan Sherman—spilled nothing dirtier than lines like Lehrer's Boy Scout meeting a Girl Scout: "Don't be nervous, don't be flustered, don't be scared / Be prepared." Holding ourselves to the same standards, we enjoyed hearing ten- or twelve-year-old kids come up to us after shows and boast how they'd memorized all our songs. But in 1998, when young kids hustled up to us reciting "I'm unzippin' my doodah, every day," our parental side left us muttering to ourselves, *"Oh please, don't behave like the president."*

Right around this time, our number of shows for high school or majority-teen audiences began to skyrocket. Through our two decades, we've done hundreds of fundraisers for public and private schools in the Washington, D.C., area, often raising money for very wholesome causes like booze-free, smoke-free, sex-free graduation parties. So now we found ourselves arriving in high school auditoria, singing semi-salacious songs about the president, knowing full well that if he (and we) were high school kids who did (or joked in a show) about these things, we'd almost surely get suspended, humiliated in the local papers, rejected by top colleges, and see our very lives crash down on our naughty heads.

But he did it, and we sang about it. And those audiences laughed—including deans, principals, parents. The kids did too, usually, though we sometimes heard afterwards how teens in our high school shows were amazed that we said and did *that* on their pristine stages. Most were amazed-pleased, but a few were amazed-not.

These teens had been born in the 1980s, part of the new, post-X, Millennial Generation. For them, to that point, Bill Clinton was the only U.S. president they'd ever known. Polls revealed America's late-'90s teens to have viewed Clinton's behavior far more harshly than adults. Yet, whether they liked the president or not, nearly all teens roared when our performer playing Clinton strode on stage, blowing kisses at the girls, we'd hear plenty of teens holler "We love you, Bill" or give the *Wayne's World* "we're not worthy" bow. "I couldn't believe what I was hearing," recalls Mark Eaton, who played that role at many a teen show. "Then again, Clinton kind of lived his life like a teenager—screwing up, getting caught doing things he wasn't supposed to, and then saying he was sorry when he knew, and you knew, he was going to do it again the next time no one was looking."

In the late '90s, three organizations (the National Youth Leadership Conference, Presidential Classroom, and Close-Up) ran programs enabling high-achieving, civics-minded high school students to visit the nation's capital, watch the House and Senate in session, see the monuments and museums, and get an up-close-and-personal government lesson.

Much as we might have approached three groups of investment bankers, we asked all three of these groups if they'd be willing to shift one evening's entertainment from area dinner theaters (the kids, we assured them, could see *Oklahoma* back home in Tulsa) to political satire. These were tightly chaperoned programs, jittery of receiving complaints from moms and dads, so we promised a squeaky-geeky super-G show. All three programs liked the idea, on the premise that, at best, our show would be educational—or, at least, would provide a little mid-week fun in between bus rides.

So, on the verge of Monica, we started doing several dozen shows per year for large crowds of visiting teens. Like they say: in comedy, timing is everything.

At first, we weren't sure what the response would be—after all, some of us had been surly teens ourselves, but these audiences were just great from day one. Some songs—like EuroPest, our ever-popular parody of "Be My Guest"—worked even better for kids than for adults. Yet, in the late '90s, some teenagers could be totally stringent politically correct police. In what felt like a cartoon of the Culture War, a teenage foursome once complained to us bitterly, after a youth show, about how incredibly insensitive that song was to the French. Usually, when people make complaints, you listen. Then there are those times, like this, when you smile and nod, smile and nod, until they go away.

Our biggest teen hit, in our Super-G days, was a song about Barney the Dinosaur, set to an Irish folk song ("Christmas in Killarney") and though nearly none of the teens knew the original song, they hated that dinosaur. When our soprano soloist came out, joined by an axe-wielding hooded executioner clutching Barney's head in a noose, teen crowds erupted. ("It's I love you / And you love

 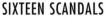

me / This creature is drivin' me up a tree / It's time for killing Barney.") At the end of the song, when the executioner lopped off Barney's head, we'd get a cheer of vicious vengeance, on the order of what Marie Antoinette would have heard, had her ears worked a few seconds longer.

We knew teenagers were well aware of Chelsea Clinton's dilemma. It's one thing to have mom and dad lurking around when you're watching TV downstairs, with the door open. It's quite another thing to have the Secret Service. So, to "Barbie Girl," we put our Chelsea in a curly red wig and had her sing: "I'm a Chelsea girl / In a Stanford world / How fantastic / How monastic / You can't touch my hair / Or undress me anywhere / No cohabitation / Daddy runs the nation."

Through audience reactions that ranged from colossal to zero from song to song, we learned a few facts of life about teenage humor. In particular, we learned the (partial) truth of a comment ascribed to Lenny Bruce, that it's a huge challenge for any comedian to reach an audience more than ten years younger. Nearly two decades into our tenure, nearly all our cast had reached an age closer to parents than to teens themselves. This led us to conduct a careful study of contemporary adolescence, leading to the following cultural imperative: our list of ten things that made Clinton-era teenagers laugh. They were, in order:

1. Sex
2. Goofball characters
3. Sex
4. Stupid pop stars
5. Sex
6. Anything (pick any two) about girls, boys, clothes, and food
7. Sex
8. Nasty references about home towns
9. Sex
10. Adults behaving like total idiots on stage

★★★★★★★★★★★★★★★

16 Funniest World Leaders, Since 1980

1. Boris Yeltsin
2. Saddam Hussein
3. Prince Charles
4. Yassir Arafat
5. Robert Mugabe
6. Manuel Noriega
7. Osama bin Laden
8. Vladimir Putin
9. Jacques Chirac
10. Deng Xiaoping
11. Pope John Paul II
12. Imelda Marcos
13. Tony Blair
14. Boutros-Boutros Ghali
15. Muammar Qaddafi
16. Mikhail Gorbachev

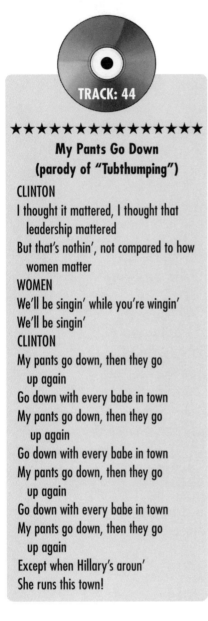

★★★★★★★★★★★★★★★

**My Pants Go Down
(parody of "Tubthumping")**

CLINTON
I thought it mattered, I thought that
   leadership mattered
But that's nothin', not compared to how
   women matter
WOMEN
We'll be singin' while you're wingin'
We'll be singin'
CLINTON
My pants go down, then they go
   up again
Go down with every babe in town
My pants go down, then they go
   up again
Go down with every babe in town
My pants go down, then they go
   up again
Go down with every babe in town
My pants go down, then they go
   up again
Except when Hillary's aroun'
She runs this town!

Our difficulty in addressing the five odd-numbered items on this list constrained us somewhat, given our premise that we could actually entertain teenagers by presenting G-rated shows.

Along came Monica. Here was one name in the news they knew, right away. She was maybe a half-dozen years older than they were—and maybe a half-dozen years less mature than they were. Thanks to this girl in the blue beret, the Oval Office had become the sort of place where adults did the kinds of things described in the nasty notes they remembered from their middle-school years. What red-blooded teenager, boy or girl, wouldn't want to laugh at *that?*

After the scandal broke, we kept the teen shows the same—for awhile. The teen-show program counselors watched us limp through a few rather tame Monica-free shows, then admitted: Clinton did it, the kids all know every exquisite detail, it's the big news story of the year, our show makes no sense without it, no parent can possibly complain that a political comedy show includes it, so go for it. Which we did.

Predictably, the teen crowds loved any and every Clinton libido moment we tossed them.

We then learned another crucial lesson about teen humor, as applied to parodies. Up to now, nearly all our songs were of our own teen era, if not before. We had precious little from the '90s—or '80s. Mostly boomers ourselves, we had seldom parodied the songs that flavored the Gen-X high school and college years. Weird Al Yankovich did numerous parodies of Gen-X tunes, his jokes arising more from the MTV videos than the words. Not having done any videos, we had to rely on words, and not so many songs of that era had the kind of hook needed to write parodies in our style. Those songs that did have a hook were utterly unknown to most people our age and older.

The late '90s were different. More of the songs lent themselves to parodies, and people our age (aka parents of teenagers) actually knew some of them.

A pop tune by Chumbawumba gave us our breakthrough youth song. The core lyric—"I get knocked down / Then I get up again"— translated wonderfully into "My pants go down / Then they go up again," and more. During the first week of the Lewinsky scandal, we introduced that song in our teen shows, with great results.

That set us down the path looking for pop tunes of the kids' own era. We used the Spice Girls' pop lyric "So tell me what you like / What you really really like" to press an argument between Monica and Linda Tripp ("So tell me what you did / What you really really did / He went an' / Huh? / He went an' / Huh? / He went an' / Huh? / He went an' / Huh? / He went an' really really really went unzip-unzip, ah!").

"I Believe I Can Fly" became Clinton's answer to Ken Starr: "I believe I can lie / I believe I can stiff this guy / I get subpoenaed every night and day / I make up things and just lie away." Shaggy's "It Wasn't Me" became our Clinton's ode for denying the affair to a nagging reporter. ("Heard you did it in the hallway / It wasn't me / Heard she did it with you all day / It wasn't me.")

Writing for teens offers a very different challenge, quite unlike writing for adults. Puns and clever lyrics count for very little. "If the song rates high enough on the hip factor for kids," notes Mark Eaton, who has written several, "they won't care what lines you sing, because they won't hear them. They'll all be screaming."

You can tell right away with teenagers if they know a song. Once the music starts, there's a buzz of recognition, almost like a game show, as various kids try to show off that they could figure out the tune before anybody else. Adult crowds, faced with the same situation, merely grin and nod when they recognize a tune. For performers, you can imagine which kind of show is more fun to do.

Since then, we added all kinds of teen-pop tunes, to a degree we never dared try back in the 1980s and early '90s. We did an Animal Planet routine ridiculing fast food, home states, and teen stereotypes. We even stooped to producing our own Britney Spears, *Oops*-ing over the loss of secret files, Palm Beach ballots, you-name-it. The subject didn't matter, as long as the bust was big enough, the voice breathy-warbly enough, and the character stupid enough.

The rise of George W. Bush coincided with the rise of boy bands, which perhaps is more than mere coincidence. We replaced our adult "I Wanna Be Like You, George" duet of George Senior and Junior ("Cat's Cradle" being sweet to boomer ears but totally foreign and middle-agey to their teenage kids) with a parody of the Backstreet Boys's hit "I Want it That Way," altered ever so slightly to "I Want It Dad's Way." Worked like a charm.

We then introduced "It's the G.O.P.," a takeoff on 'N Sync's "It's Gonna Be Me." That worked well enough on the tune alone, especially during a mid-song rap with Bush and Cheney ("Yeah, you know me / I'm G.W.B. / And I followed my daddy to the presidency" to which our overstuffed, bald-wigged Cheney, borrowing from Eminem's "The Real Slim Shady," responded, "Yes, I'm the real Cheney / All those other guys are soft just like John McCain-y").

Good so far, but when we added some dance moves, our obvious dancing limitations worked to our advantage—using styles from boy band videos—swinging invisible lassos, jumping in place, signature hand gestures. The teens loved it. "Kids don't want to see middle-aged people trying to act like kids," notes Eaton. "They prefer adults trying to do things kid-like, even if it isn't done very well."

When you watch today's teenagers on their own stages, in high schools, what you see is in many ways the opposite of what was going on when their boomer parents were that age. Reeling from the sappy blandness of '50s-era musicals, the kids of the '60s turned away from elaborate sets and brightly colored costumes, from tight harmonies and choreographies, from the very bigness of shows. But the teens of now are turning back to all that, with the added benefit of more singing, dancing, and acting lessons than their parents ever had, aided by greatly enhanced stage technologies.

Through the Cappies, the national high school "critics and awards" program the Capitol Steps are sponsoring, we've learned quite a lot about what today's teens do on stage. It's impressive—and illuminating.

Go to a high school show, or a one-act festival, and the humor you'll be likely to see is far more tightly planned, blocked, engineered, and

rehearsed than anything their parents ever put on in high school. A one-piece set folds into its exact opposite. A two-person dialogue snaps with perfect timing. Three doors slam at exactly the same instant. A four-person collision is gymnastic in the precision of the pratfalls. What teenagers tend to do on their own stages brings to mind a modern meld of Lucille Ball and Red Skelton, a fresh remake of a genre of humor that felt old to their parents back in the '60s.

Think Amanda Bynes and Frankie Muniz times many, singing, dancing, and getting laughs in big choreographed shows in schools all over the United States, and you get the picture.

Thus does the American sense of humor continue to evolve, from one generation to the next. When we travel the country doing our show, we constantly run into audience members who first saw us as high school students visiting Washington. The fact that they came back to see us gives us hope. Maybe we weren't total dorks, and maybe they *were* laughing (and screaming) *with* us.

Sure, today's teens "want it dad's way," but they're also learning to do it *their* way. Rest assured: the American capacity to laugh, and the interest in political satire, is alive and well in this next generation.

We can only imagine what jokes they'll someday write about their own leaders, and what shows they'll someday perform for their own teenage kids. What the Capitol Steps have done with on-stage song parody, they might do through broadband downloads, or interactive technologies, or other joke devices that haven't been invented yet. Whichever, today's fans of Nickelodeon and MTV are the scandal-makers and scandal-breakers of tomorrow.

And, let's hope, we'll still be around to catch the punch, feel the heat, and share the laugh.

15

Y2K & E2K
("I Want a Brand New Pair of Candidates")

★★★★★★★★★
TRACKS: 45–48

Abraham Lincoln liked to tell the story of sages who, upon being asked by a weary king for a truism that would apply to all times and things, good or bad, replied, "This too shall pass away."

The Clinton scandals had to end. Likewise the Clinton presidency. And, with it, the national mood—and comic attitude—that had accompanied all that. We had entered the *fin de siécle*, the final gasps of the twentieth century.

For awhile, it seemed as if the Clinton scandals, like the man himself, would never go away. No sooner had his impeachment trial ended in acquittal than we had to endure the spectacle of a U.S. president entering his "repentant" stage—mostly, he was sorry he

got caught. Now, the key joke was how he'd deal with Hillary. Our 1999 album cover, "First Lady and the Tramp," portrayed Bill sucking up a spaghetti straw that led straight to Hillary. The last straw.

Republicans had to go off-scandal, cold turkey, and actually talk about budget policy again. Apologies to Dorothy and Toto, but "Let's get over the bimbos, G.O.P." In this political Land of Oz, the munchkins were getting a little nervous. ("Some days I wish that Kenneth Starr / Would see how things have gone too far, like hello / The speaker cheated on his spouse / Now other members of the House have knees of Jell-O.")

That winter, America went a little goofball. A number of people took a break from routine and went on little outings. Like Ellen DeGeneres. Thanks to Larry Flynt, many a Republican was rumored to have an "outing" of one sort or another. We felt a celebration was in order, so we parodied the lively "Shout" song ("And so this woman's coming *out!* / Of the closet, I am *out!* / Jerry Falwell, come on *out!* / Pat Buchanan, you come *out!* / We need, now / Ralph Reed, now / Hey-ey-ey-ey / J. Edgar Hoover, he was gay…").

Minnesotans created satire by the buckets when they elected the fun Governor Jesse "My party can beat up your party" Ventura. ("You've gotta know when to hold 'em / Know when to fold 'em / Know when to body slam / And how to whip their butts / Tell those Gores and Quayles and Bushes / I'll kick your prissy tushes.") We joined Jesse with Ross "the Boss" Perot in a dream team that, we think, may have inspired the XFL.

None of these diversions succeeded in directing the subject away from the debris of the Clinton scandals, in part because the president's defenders persisted in wanting to attacking his attackers. *Thank you, thank you, just keep this story alive,* every comedian in America was silently thinking, as Clinton's chums tried to prosecute Linda Tripp and kept arguing over what might or might not be in the special prosecutor's final report.

Only one man could change the news—Clinton himself—and he did so brilliantly. Surely, he'd been inspired by the film *Wag the Dog*, with its astonishingly prescient prophecy of a U.S. president who had a seamy affair with a girl in a beret and then saved his derriere by launching a little war in some silly little country in, to pick a place at random, the Balkans.

For years, Clinton had contented himself with lobbing a few ham sandwiches to the Bosnians, Croats, Albanians, and others who'd been battling the Serbs. The most aggressive action our forces had taken up to then had been when a pilot, Scott O'Grady, got shot down, had to hide in a ditch and eat worms and spiders until he got rescued at the cost of tens of millions of dollars, and then came home to the awaiting arms of Katie Couric and a book agent. Sure, we got a song out of it ("I'm in the Mood for Bugs") but these limited military actions weren't bringing peace in the former Yugoslavia.

Freed from Senate Republicans, Clinton was ready to show an easier nemesis—the Serbs—that he meant business. Our president was starting to obsess about his legacy. (We imagined him wondering, "Will there be a statue of me erected?") He had entered his Nobel Search Phase, and he desperately needed a way to carve out at least one sentence in history books with words that didn't rhyme with unbreechment. He focused like a laser beam, bit his lip real hard, and thought he could unravel centuries of blood feuds in a particularly nasty corner of the world.

The American people were genuinely confused about what the historical reasons for this could possibly be. When no serious answer makes any sense, it's time to offer an *unserious* one, which we did, in a parody of "Dry Bones," speedily delivered by our own Professor Slobydam Sonovavich: "A Serb bought five sheep in a medieval store / Express line that had a limit of four / Kosovar said, 'That's too many sheep' / Serb called Kosovar a hairy creep / Kosovar swung, and he hit Croat / Croat swung back and he knocked Serb flat / Serb said, 'Croat, 'cuz-a what you've done / My great grandkid will start World War I' / Croat said, 'Beware of World War II / And what my great great grandkid'll do to you' / Serb said, 'I'll bet my family kin / In the 1990s gonna do yours in' / And that's what led to the war."

To correct this as surgically as possible, American jets surgically dropped precision bombs on Yugoslavia from oh, somewhere around

500,000 feet in the air, cratering within oh, a few miles of the actual target. (Close only counts in horseshoes and carpet bombing.) We trotted out our own Kosovar tour guide to describe his country's many fine attractions to the tune of the Beach Boys's "Kokomo." ("Come visit Tiblisi / The food is very greasy / The women in Ustach / Are famous for their moustache / The guys in Pristina / Have teeth like a hyena / Plumbing like long ago / Way down in Kosovo.")

Kosovars desperately wanted Clinton to send in ground troops, but that was too risky for this U.S. president, given his own war record. Instead, U.S. planes bombed the Chinese Embassy. Our Bill Clinton called the Chinese to apologize because, after all, the killing of innocent Chinese civilians was normally the job of the Chinese military. *Ooh.* That one got a nervous laugh from some crowds, perhaps because U.S.-China relations were fraying badly. The Chinese were suspected of stealing our nuclear secrets. But, it turned out, they didn't steal them. They paid good money for them.

Clinton's *Wag the Dog* war turned out pretty well. Actually, he pitched a shutout, zero U.S. combat casualties. It took him seven long years, but at long last the man succeeded in getting sex—his and everybody else's—off the front pages.

For the rest of the year, the funniest news involved a Brooklyn museum exhibit featuring feces on a painting ("Dung at Art"), a space probe to Mars that got lost because an aerospace contractor had actually gotten inches mixed up with millimeters ("Blame it on the Boss at NASA"), and a lot of hoohah about a "millennium bug" that ended up biting with the fury of a dead millipede. Quite a folly that the U.S. government spent all those billions protecting us from what *didn't* strike in Y2K, instead of protecting us from what *did* in Y2K+1.

These and other "who cares" issues were comedic game in those loopy last months of the Clinton era because, though petty, they passed the water cooler test—that is, they had "buzz." But, somehow, they lacked the old pizzazz. Americans were too used to thong jokes, and the Lewinsky scandals were a tough act to follow. Telling topical jokes in the wake of the most heavily publicized—and laughed at—sex scandal in human history was like trying to inflate a used balloon. You could still do it, but it just wasn't as much fun as before.

For awhile, the 2000 presidential elections looked like an incredibly dreary affair, between two daddy's boys with familiar faces and old ideas. That was *until* Dan Quayle announced he was gearing up for a presidential bid. We gleefully trotted out all our tried-and-true Dan jokes (like how he agreed to submit to an IQ test, because he was sure the results would come back negative), but this time all the comedic quips took a toll. When he tanked in the first caucus, the real Dan dropped out of the race. ("After finishing last in Iowa, a lot of people said Dan Quayle would come home with his tail between his legs. Well, let me tell you that Dan Quayle came home with nothing between his legs.") When we heard the news, we sobbed openly on stage.

Another fun story emerged when Hillary began her run for the New York Senate seat. She needed to learn to talk like a New Yorker, so we exploited the fish-out-of-water comic angle in "I'm Just a Girl Who Can't Say Yo." *Hey, fuggeddabbouddit!* When we did our Off-Broadway show that year, we did an *Evita* overlay, "Hill'rita," with our girl miraculously transformed from carpetbagger to queen. ("All through Bill's wild days / His mad existence / I kept the power / He kept his distance.") Meanwhile, her husband salivated over his new freedom, unleashing his "La Vida Loca" as "Libido Loco."

The president was chafing, watching his vice president struggle out of the gate. Bill Bradley was breathing down his neck—literally. Our Dollar Bill dressed in a seven-foot outfit buttressed by large coat-hangers, in which he sang "I Got Arrhythmia." ("Got my heartbeat / And you know that's certainly more / Than you'd ever get with Al Gore.") Bradley's secret strategy was to be even more boring than Gore. Brilliant move.

According to rumor, Gore had once claimed to have invented the Internet. Whether true or not, this was amusing because it deftly fit his

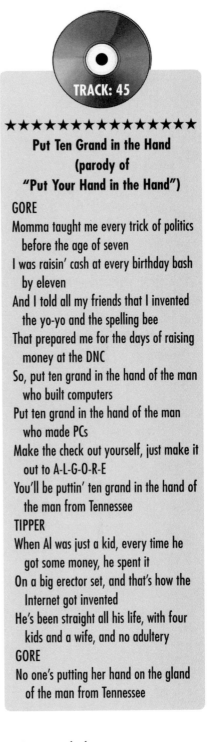

TRACK: 45

★★★★★★★★★★★★★★★★★

**Put Ten Grand in the Hand
(parody of
"Put Your Hand in the Hand")**

GORE
Momma taught me every trick of politics
  before the age of seven
I was raisin' cash at every birthday bash
  by eleven
And I told all my friends that I invented
  the yo-yo and the spelling bee
That prepared me for the days of raising
  money at the DNC
So, put ten grand in the hand of the man
  who built computers
Put ten grand in the hand of the man
  who made PCs
Make the check out yourself, just make it
  out to A-L-G-O-R-E
You'll be puttin' ten grand in the hand of
  the man from Tennessee
TIPPER
When Al was just a kid, every time he
  got some money, he spent it
On a big erector set, and that's how the
  Internet got invented
He's been straight all his life, with four
  kids and a wife, and no adultery
GORE
No one's putting her hand on the gland
  of the man from Tennessee

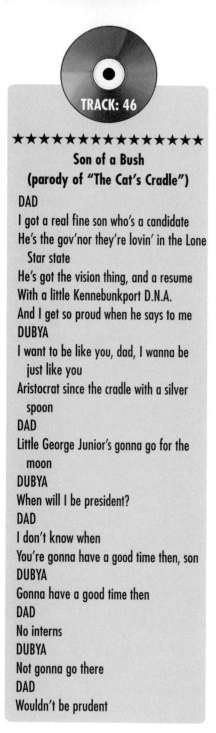

TRACK: 46

★★★★★★★★★★★★★★★

Son of a Bush
(parody of "The Cat's Cradle")

DAD

I got a real fine son who's a candidate

He's the gov'nor they're lovin' in the Lone
Star state

He's got the vision thing, and a resume

With a little Kennebunkport D.N.A.

And I get so proud when he says to me

DUBYA

I want to be like you, dad, I wanna be
just like you

Aristocrat since the cradle with a silver
spoon

DAD

Little George Junior's gonna go for the
moon

DUBYA

When will I be president?

DAD

I don't know when

You're gonna have a good time then, son

DUBYA

Gonna have a good time then

DAD

No interns

DUBYA

Not gonna go there

DAD

Wouldn't be prudent

know-it-all persona. Before, he was the guy who told the teacher they forgot to collect the homework— now, he was the guy who took credit for your homework. An accomplished fundraiser, Gore was shown the money in every imaginable kind of place, including a Buddhist Temple (a "tudist bemple" with "nudist buns"). While fat-cat Democrats were summoned to "Put Ten Grand in the Hand of the Man from Tennessee," we celebrated his un-Clintonian virtue by singing, "He's led a straight life, with four kids and a wife, and no adultery / No one's puttin' her hand on the gland of the man from Tennessee."

Ah, Tipper. And "The Kiss" that propelled Fast Albert into the lead, proving that America's women think it's OK (even a good thing) for a man to be a little stiff. We had been waiting for years, and finally we had some sexy way to tease dear Al. ("And now he leads / The White House race / Since that night, at our convention / When you saw us sucking face / I should have laid down on the stage / And let him make sweet love to me / To let you see how Al's positions / Differ from the G.O.P.")

Gore's choice for Veep was Joe Lieberman, a devout Jew, who promised to devote himself to a workaholic campaign, 24/6. ("One goy / one special goy / To go and schmooze with / To snooze with / To lose with.")

The other "goy" in the race—George Dubya Bush— was just another "Cat's Cradle" wild and crazy guy all grown up and sobered down, with family mansions in Texas and Maine ("Aristocrat since the cradle with a silver spoon"), who got along so well with his dad, he wanted to grow up to be just like him ("When I can I be president? / I don't know when / You're gonna have a good time then, son / Gonna have a good time then").

Apart from pleasing his dad, Americans wondered, why was Dubya running? Was it a self-help thing, a midlife rehab project to keep a once-wayward young man on the wagon? Issues? What issues? "Read My Lips, No New Issues"—prompting our song "You're so vague / We just don't know a darn thing about you."

In the early primaries, John McCain gave Dubya a real run for his soft and hard money. The Arizona Senator wasn't easy to barb, except for his over-the-top temper. To "Who'll Stop the Rain," our Bush sang "He's a hero / I'm a zero / Who'll stop McCain?"—but the race was over by the time McCain developed enough of a profile to be joke bait.

The nomination was handed to Bush the same way as his Yale degree, in a stroll down privilege lane. Even though he'd run a highly successful campaign, the public perception arose—wonder why?—that he was lighter upstairs than in the wallet. In our "Who Wants to Be a Millionaire Candidate" take-off of Regis Philbin's quiz show, we asked Dubya "The president of France is the leader of what country?" The perplexed guest asked him to repeat the question before taking a stab. Was that his *final* answer? Well, no. He did have a few lifelines left, most of them with dad's old staffers. ("I'm cheek to jowl / With Colin Powell / In the back of our big chauffeured Caddie / Won't he be great / As head of State / 'Cuz my staff belongs to Daddy.")

For vice president, he picked old frumpy but reliable "Everyone Knows It's Cheney," daddy's ex-Sec-Def, who hung onto power with steel cables but hung onto life by a thread. ("With Cheney I could go far / I'll have to learn CPR.") From day one, the key joke was about Cheney running the show for sonny-boy. Were Bush elected, he would be just a heartbeat away from the presidency.

Here was the choice: "Gush and Bore. Deedle-twee and deedle-twum." Both boomers. Both white males. Both Ivy Leaguers who got low grades. Both sons of famous political daddies. Neither could dance a lick. One had a blonde wife, the other a brunette. Hey, at least we had *some* diversity.

Their three debates weren't Lincoln-Douglas historic, or Kennedy-Nixon sober, but Abbott-Costello funny. Dubya played the straight man against Mean Al, then Nice Al, then Medium Al. *Saturday Night Live* captured him perfectly each week—first snickering behind Bush's back, then agreeing with everything he said, then somewhere in between, not sure at all what to do. The stakes were high, because the American people were watching…football.

TRACK: 47

★★★★★★★★★★★★★★★★

**I Want a Brand New
Pair of Candidates
(parody of
"Brand New Pair of Roller Skates")**

I stayed up late to watch 'em countin' the
votes
While all the networks were rescindin'
their quotes
At first, it went for Gore, and then it
goes to Bush
Forget that recount, I've got a new plan
to push
Well, I want a brand new pair of
candidates
I'd say they both have lost
I want to hold a new election
I'd gladly pay the cost
Tell 'em in Nashville and Austin
I don't like what I've seen
Oh, find me a brand new pair of
candidates
Someone like Martin Sheen

People were also watching the talk shows—Oprah, Rosie, Katie, Conan, Jay, Dave, Chris, Larry—where a guest appearance by a candidate, spouse, or surrogate, was expected to include at least some light material. Gore Democrats had the advantage here, whether from media bias or from their own greater comfort zone in this medium. When a talk show host likes or dislikes you, everyone in the world knows it. But, balancing this out, people listened to talk shows—Rush Limbaugh, Don Imus, Art Bell, and a long list of others who likewise mixed the serious with the light, and Bush Republicans definitely had the clear edge here. Each side was learning to use humor as a political weapon.

As election day approached, the polls were very close: zero to zero. ("Oh, find me a brand new pair of candidates.") People cheered at that line, plainly agreeing with the sentiment. This was our fifth presidential election as satirists, and we'd never heard audiences so hostile to *both* candidates.) Bowing to the true new god of politics, both Bush and Gore made their final pre-election appearances on a comedy show. As Peggy Noonan perceptively wrote at the time, "We are entertaining ourselves to death in America, and one of the signs and expressions of this is the fact that we don't want to pick a president who doesn't entertain us." Yes, political satire had definitely come of age with these two.

Then came election day. Election night. Election week. Election month. Florida, comedians love you. Thank you thank you *thank you* for producing the funniest election this side of Zimbabwe and Reese Witherspoon.

Were Palm Beach voters sympathetic, moronic, or comic? Probably a little of all three. In our show, a little old Florida lady, clutching a *Voting for Dummies* book, staggered out of a polling place singing "There's a hole in the center of the ballot." To which Pat Buchanan answered, "What I adore is, the hole for Al Gore is above me / Oh my darlings /

Punch three times on your ballot to support me," followed by "the Swinging Chads" (apologies to Diana Ross) their heads in white cardboard squares. ("Come to the poll, why don't you babe / Punch my hole, why don't you babe / But you never detach me / You just keep me hanging on.")

The "E2K" election turned out to be everything "Y2K" was not: an expensive ruinous mess—and very funny. All the old Culture War arguments were laid bare for all to see, memorialized by the *USA Today's* map dividing America into a vast Bush "redzone" edged by slivers of Gore "bluezone," everywhere bordered by water. The two zones reminded us of the map, and ethnic alibis, our Dr. Slobydam Sonovavich had used to describe Yugoslavia. Americans were learning that the word "balkanize" could apply to this country too.

In mid-December, the political morass *cum* comic extravaganza was climaxed by a five-to-four vote of the U.S. Supreme Court. The election was officially over, but the arguments—and jokes—were not. We chided the winners in a Supreme Court set-piece in which, thanks to costumer Linda Rose Payne, four performers portrayed the other eight justices singing "How Do You Solve a Problem Like Scalia?"—celebrating an electoral process people would be proud of. In North Korea.

With Dubya the winner, kind of sort of, we bid farewell to Bill Clinton, truly a bittersweet moment for our industry. Our Clinton character sang two Sinatra reminiscence songs, parodies of "It Was a Very Good Year" and "My Way." ("Yes, I stood tall / I chased 'em all / Don't care what they weigh.")

The real Bill gave us a final gift, even as he stubbed his toe on his way out the White House gate by pardoning a Swiss megamillionaire and removing more than just himself from the White House pantry. ("Wick Slillie was whacking the site house. He not only klept around, he was a

TRACK: 48

★★★★★★★★★★★★★★★
There's a Hole in the Center of the Ballot (parody of "There's a Hole at the Bottom of the Sea")

There's a hole in the center of the ballot
There's a hole in the center of the ballot
There's a hole, there's a hole, there's a hole in the center of the ballot
And, we've made this easy for our vision-impaired voters
There's some braille near the tiny little pointer near the name to the left of the arrow near the name to the right of the hole in the center of the ballot
There's a riot in the streets and a guy on TV and a Jesse on the march and a judge in the court near the braille near the tiny little pointer near the name to the left of the arrow near the name to the right of the hole in the center of the ballot
There's a hole, there's a hole
There's a hole in the center of our heads

TRACK: 48

★★★★★★★★★★★★★★★★★

**Singing Chads
(parody of
"You Keep Me Hanging On" and
"Who Let the Dogs Out?")**

Come to the poll, why don't you babe
Poll
Punch my hole, why don't you babe
Hole
But you never detach me
You just keep me hanging on
Who punched the chads out? Who who
who who who?

sleptomaniac.") We heard the rumor—and, in comedy, all rumors are presumed correct unless proven false beyond a reasonable doubt—that outgoing Clinton staffers removed the *W*s from all White House computer keyboards. In our show, George Blank Bush demanded to know "hen, here, hy, and ho" this happened.

Upon arriving in New York, the ex-president wanted fancy digs in midtown Manhattan, but was ridiculed for the cost, so he moved to Harlem. As usual, our Clinton was quick with a rogue's alibi. ("When I was looking for a location for my office, I was hoping to find something Jeffersonian. But I was kinda thinking Thomas, not George and Weezie.") It gave us our final Clinton-as-Elvis song, "In the Ghetto," while our newly retired Clinton also offered some advice to the lovelorn. Like Jesse Jackson, going through a paternity mess. ("What brand did you use for protection? Firestone?")

Whatever our views as citizens, we were sad as comedians to see this giant target sink into obscurity. At first, we weren't sure about the amusement potential of our new president. Dubya's frequent mangling of the English language kept us salivating over each news conference. ("To bring this country together, we need a bipartisan coagulation.") Otherwise, though, the new president struck us as recycled joke material, equal parts his dad and Dan Quayle, with a little urban cowboy thrown in. Laura Bush looked to be the least funny first lady of our lifetime. How do you make a joke out of smiling all the time, being sweet, reading books to little kids?

Then Vice President Dick Cheney had a pacemaker implanted. Funny? Not necessarily, unless you send someone out dressed up in a giant foam heart to deliver his "Angina Monologues." But you can only take health jokes so far.

In those first hundred days, Bush's Cabinet seemed utterly immune to comedy—except for John Ashcroft, named Attorney General because Dubya knew he was (apologies to *Fiddler on the Roof*) "pro-life, pro-life, like I am / Like I am, like I am, pro-life." The perception that Ashcroft opposed sex because it could lead to dancing…seemed credible. And Gail Norton, who rumor had it was basically James Watt in a dress, gave us the opportunity to bring back our Reagan-era parody, "Mine Every Mountain."

The new president had to work with a Senate split 50-50, making the health of Strom Thurmond crucial to the balance of power. Our old Quayle-era song "Stayin' Alive" morphed into "Keep Him Alive." Then Vermonter "You-Don't-Mess-Around-With" Jim Jeffords tipped the balance of power in a bold move that may have fundamentally altered the shape of excruciatingly vital legislation and thereby changed forever the future of our nation—or maybe not—but, comedically, the story barely rippled.

We didn't know it at the time, of course, but that summer of 2001 was comedy's Indian Summer, the last dash of lazy warmth before a sharp chill soon to come. It was that for the nation, too. The evenings were pleasantly cool in D.C., luckily for our male cast, because an epidemic of British dairy disease put us once more into those cow suits. ("We had joy, we had fun / We had lesions on our gums.")

Ah, for those good old days, the tail end of the '90s, back when tourists visited the White House, nobody cared what shoes you wore on planes, and Anne Heche made bigger headlines than the president.

The silliest talk was about Gary Condit, who brought to mind a Bill Clinton without the slick empathy, power wife, Oval Office penumbra, and shout-show defenders. After ducking the media for several weeks, he consented to a prime-time interview with Connie Chung on national TV. Unlike Clinton, a surly Condit showed none of the rascal's talent to charm his way out of trouble.

Through most of the 2001 summer, Condit was the closest anybody came to comic raw meat, even if his scandal was tinged with personal tragedy. We tried a lirty die, about this "Juan Don from Falicornia," but audiences were tepid. Dancing on the edge of taste, we trotted out our favorite parody tune for any and all scandals, "The Boxer," and brought out a Connie Chung and electric-haired Gary Condit. "Were you O.J. mixed with Clinton? / Were you plowing all your staff? / Tell the truth for once, and please don't make us laugh," asked our Chung, to which our Condit replied, as so many others had in our show over the years, "Lie lie-lie. Lie lie-lie-lie, lie lie-lie. Lie lie-lie…" It wasn't much, but it was all we could offer. Like the stillness of the air before a storm, the stillness of the culture made a person wonder if something new, something powerful, was over the horizon but on its way.

At the Houseman theater in New York City, up the subway from the World Trade Center, we had begun our shows by singing a parody of "The Circle of Life": "You know life isn't clean / You want dirty and mean / In a circle of lies." Well, what *did* we want?

At the Reagan Theater in Washington, D.C., up the blue line from the Pentagon, we closed our shows—on the weekend of September 8 and 9, 2001—by singing a parody of "The Impossible Dream": "This is our quest / In scandals we trust / What's bad for our country / Is good news for us." *Oh?*

That next Tuesday morning, the twentieth century was totally over. All its residual puff would soon get out of the papers, out of our show, and into the dusty files of history.

Y2K turned out to be bogus, E2K goofy. What came next would be neither.

16

God Bless America
("Which City? What City?")

★★★★★★★★★
TRACKS: 49–52

September 11, 2001. We like to joke about how, after every big news event, our first thought is to find a rhyme and a punch line. Not this time. Like other Americans, we watched with horror as events unfolded live on television.

As we did, we couldn't help but think of a song we'd performed hundreds of times over the prior two and a half years, "Pakistani Bang Bang," a parody of "Chitty Chitty Bang Bang," a satire on the spread of nuclear weapons and global terrorism. Some of its lyrics were chillingly prescient. *"Which city? What city? / L.A. or New York City? / Smuggle in some anthrax, put it in our back packs / Bang bang city-city bang-bang is coming to your town..."*

"Pakistani Bang Bang" was slated on the song list for a show scheduled for September 12. That show was canceled, and we never sang that song again.

In our own workplace, we of the Capitol Steps felt exactly the same way people did in schools, offices, and factories across America. We could drive by the Pentagon and see the path of destruction firsthand. As you might imagine, it was an odd moment to be in the comedy business, no time to poke fun at political foibles. Americans were rallying around leaders, with good reason.

The 11th was a Tuesday. By Wednesday morning, most of our private shows for September, and many for October, had been postponed or canceled. Dinners, meetings, conventions, fundraisers—the core of our schedule—nearly none of them were going forward as planned. Very few planes were flying, and those that did had nearly nobody in them. On the weekend of September 14 and 15, we had several public shows scheduled, all of which were unplugged—except one. We were under contract to do a show on Saturday, September 15, at a nightclub in Annapolis, Maryland.

We weren't sure doing a comedy show was the right thing to do following the most disastrous week of our lifetimes. All the networks were still replaying video of those two planes crashing into the World Trade Center, the buildings collapsing, and people running and crying. The next day, Sunday, had been declared a national day of mourning. But the club owner had a full house, and he felt it was important that we do the show. He wasn't alone. Many of our national leaders were urging all Americans to get back to business as usual.

We began to rewrite the show. The first job was to decide which bits were no longer tasteful. Anything mentioning war, the Middle East, or airline travel was obviously out. We carefully avoided depicting anybody as Arab. We combed the show for any references to violence or terrorism.

Beyond the need not to be tasteless, our more fundamental comedic problem was that so much of what we'd recently been joking about now seemed utterly irrelevant. A song about cloning wasn't offensive, but who was thinking about that on September 12? The luckiest man in America at this point was Gary Condit. We could still get away with poking fun at him—we thought it was quite a joke that he, of all people, was named to a select House committee on counter-terror intelligence—but by now nobody cared much about Condit, other than to want him and his seamy story off the news and out of their faces.

We approached that Annapolis show with trepidation, unsure whether anyone would show up, other than a few reporters to accuse us of horrendous taste. What happened? The room was packed—nearly everyone who had bought a ticket showed up. To start, Bill Strauss made a somber announcement about how we of the Capitol Steps shared the nation's grief, and how we hoped to provide a little laughter to help us all carry the load, performers and audience alike. And then a somewhat unexpected thing happened—the audience was great. Our cast has never appreciated a good crowd more than they did the folks who came out that night and told us by their reaction that it was OK to laugh, OK to take one's mind off the tragic events, if only for a short time. We closed the show with the whole audience standing and singing "God Bless America."

Still, the next several weeks were a minefield for comedians. *Politically Incorrect*'s Bill Maher hurt his show and reputation with a remark about the bravery of suicide bombers. Jerry Falwell stepped into a similar trap by implying that loose morals had brought this tragedy upon us. This prompted the president's press spokesman, Ari Fleischer, to warn comedians to "watch what you say, watch what you do"—a chilling reminder of how the passions of war can erode the hard-won freedoms for which we are fighting. Someday, perhaps in his memoirs, Ari will unwind that spin.

In this twenty-first century, the royal court doesn't need to tell the jesters how to behave. We knew. If we hadn't, our audiences would have told us for sure, with

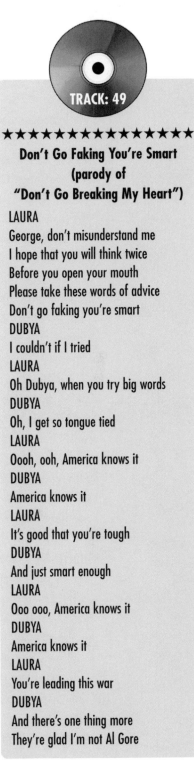

TRACK: 49

★★★★★★★★★★★★★★★

**Don't Go Faking You're Smart
(parody of
"Don't Go Breaking My Heart")**

LAURA
George, don't misunderstand me
I hope that you will think twice
Before you open your mouth
Please take these words of advice
Don't go faking you're smart
DUBYA
I couldn't if I tried
LAURA
Oh Dubya, when you try big words
DUBYA
Oh, I get so tongue tied
LAURA
Oooh, ooh, America knows it
DUBYA
America knows it
LAURA
It's good that you're tough
DUBYA
And just smart enough
LAURA
Ooo ooo, America knows it
DUBYA
America knows it
LAURA
You're leading this war
DUBYA
And there's one thing more
They're glad I'm not Al Gore

groans, hisses, complaints on the way out, and angry emails. We got none of that, in part because—as political people ourselves—we were very careful about our material. Those post 9/11 shows were a little light on the big belly laughs, but we heard many very warm post-show comments from people who told us they hadn't been sure how it was going to feel, laughing in the face of tragedy, but who found that it felt pretty good. And, in a comment unique to those weeks, they thanked us less for how funny we were than for the "care" we'd taken with our material.

We had to curtail our gibes at the current leaders—not necessarily because they weren't funny, but because now America so desperately wanted and needed them to do well at jobs that felt more vital than before. For awhile, audiences actually wanted to *applaud* their politicians—how's *that* for a new twist—so we threw them some cheer lines, poked fun at how great they were, as in "That's why the Rudy is a champ."

Given this new mood, jokes about Dick Cheney's heart didn't seem right, not with him in a bunker somewhere with a vast security apparatus safeguarding his life. Nor were our various bits questioning the intelligence or toughness of the president. We could still tease him for being like his dad, but now his old man was less "read my lips" George than Desert Storm butt-kicking George.

With Dubya's popularity soaring as Americans rallied behind him, the new joke on him was how *smart* he was. This comic take wasn't quite the same as that famous *Saturday Night Live* routine in which Phil Hartman played an alert, aggressive Ronald Reagan brilliantly micromanaging every detail of Iran-Contra. *That* was ridicule, because everybody knew Reagan wasn't like that. *This* was America hoping that Bush was, quoting a *USA Today* headline, the "same president" but a "different man."

The Dubya of our post-9/11 show revealed that he'd been hiding his high IQ because, as Al Gore demonstrated, nobody likes a know-it-all. The stupid demeanor of his past was just a "self-defecating fakade." Now, he was using his ample cerebellum to become fluent in the Afghani language, enabling him to tell Osama in his own language what was in store for him. ("What's Afghani for 'Lorena Bobbitt'?")

More than before, foreign leaders became comic—but only if they

★★

16 Funniest Scandal Quotes

1. "I've learned not to put things in my mouth that are bad for me." (Monica Lewinsky)
2. "It depends on what the meaning of 'is' is." (Bill Clinton)
3. "If it doesn't fit, you must acquit." (Johnnie Cochran)
4. "I did not have sex with that woman, Monica Lewinsky." (Bill Clinton)
5. "The bitch set me up." (Marion Barry)
6. "The attractive lady whom I had only recently been introduced to dropped into my lap....I chose not to dump her off." (Gary Hart)
7. "On occasion, I discovered I would recount conversations that simply didn't happen." (Bob Packwood, describing his diary)
8. "Yes, I am Dick Armey. And if there is a 'dick army,' Barney Frank would want to join up." (Dick Armey, R-TX)
9. "What right does Congress have to go around making laws just because they deem it necessary?" (Marion Barry)
10. "There they are. See no evil, hear no evil, and...evil." (Bob Dole, describing former presidents Carter, Ford, and Nixon)
11. "Madam Speaker, it started with the training bra, and then it came to the push-up bra; the support bra, the Wonder bra, the super bra. There is even a smart bra. Now, if that is not enough to prop up your curiosity, there is now a new bra. It is called the holster bra, the gun bra. That is right, a brassiere to conceal a hidden handgun. Unbelievable. What is next? A maxi-girdle to conceal a stinger missile?" (James Traficant, D-OH, on the floor of the U.S. Congress)
12. "You know, if I were a single man, I might ask that mummy out. That's a good-looking mummy." (Bill Clinton, looking at an Incan mummy at a museum)
13. "Can you imagine having to introduce Monica Lewinsky to your family?" (Monica Lewinsky)
14. "They don't call me Tyrannosaurus Sex for nothing." (Ted Kennedy)
15. "She can reconstruct her face, her hair, and her body, but she will always be revolting to me." (Monica Lewinsky, on Linda Tripp)
16. "When I was in England, I experimented with marijuana a time or two, and I didn't like it. I didn't inhale." (Bill Clinton)

were rock-solid allies. We pictured Tony Blair as a national heartthrob, "strong, yet sensitive, a tender Rolling Stone / Just like Maggie Thatcher, but with less testosterone." When the French joined the war effort, Mark Eaton remarked to Elaina, "Oh great. What are they going to do? Supply the surrender flags?" Hence a new song, "Yackety Yack, Jacques Chiraq," was born, with the French offering to send *both* their tanks.

TRACK: 50

★★★

Obama Sin Laden
(Lirty Dies Backwards Talk)

BILL

My stext nory is about the triggest bubblemaker of the moo nillennium.

That icked weevildoer, that mudthirsty blainiac, that scarable bumtucket.

Obama Sin Laden. What a bastardly dastard.

He's worse than Whidely Sniplash.

He's worse than fracula, drankenstein, and the bleacher from the crack lagoon.

For a tong tong lime, Obama Sin Laden was priting sitty with his jibe in Tralalabad.

Until our fecial sporces and the Lorthern Annoyance based his chutt into Bora Tora.

We tried to smast him into blithereens, with our tee-fifty-boos.

It widn't durk.

Obama, beek-a-poo, yare are woo?

Did you peek into Snakistan?

Did you ooze your way into Schmoozebekistan?

Koo hairs.

We'll tail his trail until we can throw his slut in the bammer down at Buantanamo Gay.

That duck will be one dead schmuck.

And when Obama gets to the Girly Pates, old Paint Seter is gonna samn him to Dayton.

That's even worse than Cleveland.

And for the next yillion beers, Obama, they're gonna foke your putt with bitchforks.

The Internet bristled with jokes, many of them raw and viciously anti-Islamic. A better national barometer came from late-night network comics. For a while, Jay Leno and David Letterman eased off the monologues, their guests solemn, even emotional. Dan Rather openly wept on Letterman's show. The first Leno and Letterman stabs at post-9/11 jokes tended to be on the sweetly silly and patriotic side. They totally laid off Dubya jokes until, a few weeks after the attack, Leno suggested that the president was now so popular, he didn't even have to ask Dick Cheney what he was allowed to do any more. Bush jokes were all right again, but with a lighter touch than before. We kept ours largely to what we felt we could have done with the president in the audience.

Fortunately, we could still tell all the Bill Clinton and Al Gore jokes we wanted, and audiences loved it. Was it because people were glad they weren't in charge? Or from a sense of irrelevance, that you could laugh at them since they had no fateful decisions to make? Or because Americans needed somebody, anybody, to laugh at, not leader or enemy, friend or foe, pure good or pure evil, and these two guys were about all there was? Probably, it was a little bit of all those factors.

Our show's Bill Clinton offered to do what he does best, patting down all the women in the room "for security purposes." We had him admitting that before Bin Laden, there had been terrorists operating in the Clinton White House. "Bin Lyin', Bin Cheatin', and Bin Impeached."

As the comedic mood thawed, we began taking new chances with our material. A couple of weeks after 9/11, we dropped our serious intro in favor of a kick-ass military march, led by Major Offensive, who was devastating the Taliban morale by carpet bombing Afghanistan with "Victoria's Secret Catalogues, Kathy Lee Gifford CDs, and pictures of women attending college." For another month or so, though, we kept "God Bless America" as a closer. Audiences always stood and sang, whether from true feeling or patriotic compulsion, we couldn't be sure.

In October, New York Mayor Rudy Giuliani signaled that Americans needed to loosen up a little. At a Carnegie Hall fundraiser, he mocked his own authoritarian image. "I'm here to give you permission to laugh," he told the audience. "And if you don't, I'll have you arrested."

Around the first of November, we sensed that, yes, audiences were loosening up. We shifted to a closing song that had nothing to do with politics—"Old Man Wizard," heralding thirty-eight-year-old Michael Jordan's return to basketball with our local team, while ribbing him for being old (albeit younger than most of *us*). We soon shifted to a finale that went after official Washington for the new security clampdown. With anthrax jitters, people everywhere were calling 911 if they saw residue from a powdered donut. D.C. had code red security everywhere from Reagan National airport (where you could be arrested if you stood on a plane in the first thirty minutes of flight) to the federal building where we did our public shows (where if you didn't bring a photo ID, forget it, and no refunds). Was that funny? We thought so. "Glory glory paranoia / Ain't it startin' to annoy ya? / Even junk mail can destroy ya…"

"Are we laughing yet?" *USA Today* asked in early October. Irony and satire are hard sells in wartime, but the crocuses of uncensored humor were starting to spring up again on the Internet, in talk shows, and in our own show. As that splendid Annapolis audience on September 15 taught us, Americans value the fact that we all live in a country where people can freely see (and perform) a satirical show on current events. Nothing could diminish the tragedy of what had happened on September 11, but about six weeks afterwards, we sensed that our audiences no longer felt quite so self-conscious or apologetic about laughing.

By November, we still had one problem, right at home. Our out-of-town crowds were large and rocking, but Washington, D.C., audiences remained far smaller and quieter than usual. With so many jersey barriers, fenced off areas, police barricades, and metal detectors everywhere, our neighbors were a little jittery about going downtown. Hotels, restaurants, museums, theaters—everybody in the hospitality trade was hurting. Was this the same president whose White House was closed to tourists who was telling everybody else to go back to business as usual? Please. The Congressional police even closed down the Capitol steps. (The real ones.)

While Homeland Security terror alerts were heightening the sense of threats we could do absolutely nothing about, stifling tourist trade and diminishing our hometown audiences, we answered with some "Tom Ridge Fairy Tales" of our own: "We felt it necessary to inform the first little pig that terrorists may or may not be targeting straw houses at some time in the future, even though there was nothing that a mere pig could do about this…"

We were back on the road full-scale, but for us, airline travel had become an utter nightmare. Imagine arriving at the airport with large check-in bags full of plastic knives, toy guns, and other strange props. Lines and waits were sometimes horrendous, but at least we always got to our shows—even as stories of real weapons making it through security were all over the news. In our song "Pack the Knife," we had a innocent-looking passenger being detained while pirates, Vikings, and Darth Vader were waved through. At Christmastime, realizing that no one with a long beard and baggy jacket would ever get through airport security, we sang "Santa Claus Is Coming by Ground."

Jokes about hijackings always work best when the perpetrators totally goof up and nobody gets hurt—like what happened with the shoe bomber. When Elaina heard a news clip about the shoe-bomber, she immediately thought of the musical phrase "Sh-Boom," scrambled to her oldies CD collection, found the original 1950s song, and came up with "Life can be extreme / If you've ambitions to be dead extremist kooks / And if you haven't got the money for some nukes / Here's a little scheme to start / Shoe bomb, shoe bomb, shoe bomb."

As the year ended, the Office of Comedic Information was in business. At long last, *everything* felt like fair game again—bombs, cabinet members, even guys in funny Afghani hats. ("Hello, and welcome to our terrorist school. Your normal instructor will not be here. He attempted to blow up a car and burned his lips on the exhaust pipe.") When Bush decided to keep on bombing during the Ramadan season, we sang "Who'll drop a bomb during Rama-dan-a-dan? / Who'll stop the fun of their fundamental sing-song? / Who'll drop the food on Ja-la-la-la-la-bad? / Who'll drop the bags full of Spam and ham and Ding Dongs?" We trotted out Little Orphan Afghani to sing "Osama Come Out, Tomorrow," and we launched a doubletalk tirade against "Obama Sin Laden," which we closed in "fatriotic passion": "Chee threers for the bled, right, and woo of the A.S. of U., and blod guess the American lay of wife."

Yes, political comedy, like America as a whole, was getting back to normal...well, maybe not the old normal, but some new kind of normal. Not quite so over the top, not quite so cynical, so mindless of consequences, so confirmed in our false sense of security—in other words, not quite so '90s. The era of the Great American Pleasure Palace ended on September 11, 2001, and it doesn't look likely to return any time soon.

A national sense of humor is always important, but it too must (and does) change with the times. During the Great Depression, Will Rogers brought dignity to the pathos of hard times. In World War II, the Bob Hope USO tour helped our fighting forces regroup between battles, while Charlie Chaplin eased the home-front tension by laughing at an evil enemy.

The two-decade-long postwar American high, with its boxy suburbs, gray flannel corporatism, and communist witch-hunts, was aptly and ably leavened by the cartoons of *Mad* magazine and the *New Yorker*, the songs of Pete Seeger and Tom Lehrer, and the airwave satires of Steve Allen and

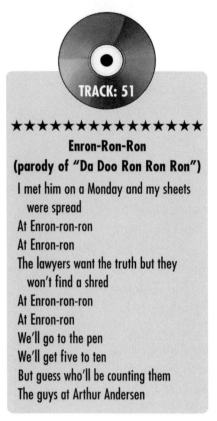

★★★★★★★★★★★★★★★★

Enron-Ron-Ron
(parody of "Da Doo Ron Ron Ron")

I met him on a Monday and my sheets
   were spread
At Enron-ron-ron
At Enron-ron
The lawyers want the truth but they
   won't find a shred
At Enron-ron-ron
At Enron-ron
We'll go to the pen
We'll get five to ten
But guess who'll be counting them
The guys at Arthur Andersen

Stan Freberg, who subtly undermined the swagger and stifle of that conformist era.

The Consciousness Revolution of the '60s and '70s needed, and got, cutting-edge satire that knocked the legs out from under "the establishment," thanks to everyone from the Smothers Brothers and Tom Paxton to Bob Dylan and the Beatles, capped by the vintage cast of *Saturday Night Live*.

Through those not quite twenty years from our first show on December 11, 1981, to that era-ending day of September 11, 2001, satire ruled, and parody flourished. In a culture rich with rivulets, individualism stood triumphant, civic life felt newly decadent, Americans felt immune from history, and everything and everyone could be treated as just a big joke.

These twenty years were the era of Comedy Central, of talking head shout shows mixing farce with analysis, of Weird Al and hiphop, of former counter-culturists making megabucks as media moguls, of ex-Congressional staffers doing political satire shows in resorts for anybody able to pay a handsome fee. Sure, we Capitol Steps were part of it too.

What will the next twenty years hold? We'll leave that to other books with other purposes, except to say: Whatever comes, we as Americans will still have the need, and (we hope) the ability, to laugh. It's one of the things that makes us glad we live here. After all, could you have done this show in Taliban-controlled Afghanistan? Well, maybe *once*.

Tragedy can always knock joy out of people and quiet the comedians—but only for awhile, because we Americans know that our sense of humor is an important part of who we are. Peace or war, boom or bust, good times or bad, we need the capacity to see our lives as individuals, and acknowledge our shared life as a nation, through prisms of realities and imaginations, truths and fictions. Humor and satire are essential, because they help us to question old answers and ask new questions. Our tears were designed by nature for grief, pain, *and* laughter. Let's never forget that.

People won't. Why not? Because, thank goodness, we're a species that will never quite get it right. Money, sex, power—they'll always be around. You know what that means: more scandals. Something new to laugh about, to release a little tension.

Sure enough, America had no sooner kicked the Taliban out of Afghanistan, then along came Enron ("I met him on a Monday and my sheets were spread / At Enron-ron-ron, at Enron-ron…") and the French figure-skating judge at the Winter Olympics ("Ooh-wah ooh-wah, what a pity / Utah has more crime than New York City"). Next week, next month, next year, there will be something else just as funny. Count on it.

What we can't automatically count on, but must steadfastly protect, is our freedom to laugh, and make others laugh, at our most powerful leaders and institutions.

TRACK: 52

★★★★★★★★★★★★★★

Superfranticunproductive-nothinglegislation-Reprise (parody of "Supercalifragilisticexpialidocious")

Supercallouslegisators, there's a place to heap them
Toss them like a pile of junk, you've got a broom to sweep them
Every new election day you've got a way to (bleep) them
But because they're funny, we are betting that you'll keep them

The freedom to make fun of serious news is incredibly precious, and we should never diminish it in the name of security, after even the grimmest of events.

There are many among us who might be tempted to do that. A poll released in early 2002 by the First Amendment Center at the U.S. Comedy Arts Festival, reported that 39 percent of those surveyed would favor government restrictions on public performance of comedy routines that make light of tragedies such as those at Oklahoma City or the World Trade Center. One person in three suggested that the First Amendment goes too far. Fortunately, a solid majority disagreed, and preferred instead to leave it to comedians—who are, after all, citizens—to apply the brakes on their own, without the government stepping in.

Our nation's war against terror was code-named "Operation Enduring Freedom" for a reason. We would do well to heed the advice of Franklin D. Roosevelt who, while leading our nation through far more perilous times, reminded the people that "the conditions for democracy and art are one."

Nowhere else can a person tweak the powerful and poke the pompous more freely than in America. In half the world, a troupe like the Capitol Steps would have ended up dead or in jail. In most of the rest, petty corruptions would have kept us from ever making a living at it. Here and only here, a playfully subversive spirit can thrive.

Humor and history are able companions. May it ever be so.

When we first started out, twenty years and sixteen scandals ago, we worried that someday all the scandals would dry up, the Congress would become quietly competent, and we would run out of material. Really. We worried about that. For about five minutes.

Acknowledgments

This book, like our show, was a lot of fun to do, forcing us to dig into the recesses of our crania for twenty years of memories, and then to find meaning in it all.

One of the meanings that leapt out at us was the huge number of people who have been part of the Capitol Steps extended family over the years, the people who share credit for having gotten us rolling and keeping us going. As anyone who's ever been in the entertainment industry knows, it's very unusual for a performing troupe to stay together twenty years and counting.

We recorded the audio component of this book in February 2002, at the Baird Auditorium of the Smithsonian Museum of American History. The cast included Janet Davidson Gordon (featured as Lorena Bobbitt, Tipper Gore), Anne Willis Hill (Marilyn Quayle, Laura Bush), Mike Thornton (George Bush Sr., Bob Dylan), Mike Tilford (Bill Clinton, Ronald Reagan), Jamie Zemarel (Al Gore, George Bush Jr.), and keyboardist Howard Breitbart. Your coauthors are the narrators, with Elaina also the PC woman and elderly voter, and Bill doing the "lirty dies" spoonerisms. The sound recording is by Jim Smith of Muddy Hole Studios, with help from our own technician Greg Hammon.

To put together this book, we thank our relentless editor at Sourcebooks, Deb Werksman, whose own experience with *The Quayle Quarterly* aided immeasurably with the concept for this book. From one month to the next, with patience here and urgency there, Deb pushed us hard, and usefully so, to get the CD script and book text just right. We also thank publisher Dominique Raccah, whose MediaFusion series is uniquely visionary in the book industry. Think of all the many other books whose readers would have loved to have had a CD of music, author readings, and further commentary. Now, thanks to Dominique, that path is well set.

More broadly, there are so many people we'd like to thank, for helping the Capitol Steps through these twenty years. First off, we must acknowledge the dedication, hard work, and many fine talents of our current cast, Brian Ash, Bari Biern, Howard Breitbart, Mike Carruthers, Andy Clemence, Kevin Corbett, Nancy Dolliver, Mark Eaton, Janet Davidson Gordon, Anne Willis Hill, Marc Irwin, Ann Johnson, David Kane, Porter Koontz, Mike Loomis, Richard Paul, Linda Rose Payne, Jack Rowles, Ann Schmitt, Emily Bell Spitz, Tracey Stephens, Mike Thornton, Mike Tilford, Brad Van Grack, Delores King Williams, Lenny Williams, and Jamie Zemarel. We would also like to thank our cast, especially Mark Eaton, for their many songs and jokes.

We recognize the many fine contributions of our former cast members, including Jim Aidala, Karen Anderson, Bo Ayars, Nancy Baskin, Danny Binstock, Toby Blackwell, John Bosma, Winthrop Cashdollar, Aetna Thompson-Collins, Eileen Cornett, Patrick Cribben, Sandy Darley, Karen Doyne, Michael Forrest, Alan Friedman, Dave Gencarelli, Helen Gleason, Barbie Granzow, Duncan Hollomon, Ken Jackson, Jan Johns, Mary Joyce, J.J. Kaczynski, Adam Karsten, Toby Kemper, Kevin Kirkpatrick, Chris Manion, Cindy McDowell, Debbi Morello, David Nacht, Dave Nichols, Hal Probus, Sonya Pleasant Roth, Ken Rynne, Dave Werner, and Amy Felices Young. And we give a Capitol Steps hug to the fine family of the late Tyjuana Morris, a gifted performer and wonderful, loving woman whom we all miss so much.

To put on seven thousand shows has involved quite a lot of planning and arranging, from the old days of paper shuffling to the post-postmodern days of emailing, eticketing, e-budgeting, and e-lunching. We thank our current office helpers Brian Ash, Lisa Burns, Laura Carrano, Mike Carruthers, Mark Eaton, Greg Hammon, Bill Hurd, Linda Rose Payne, Mary Payne Omohundro, Brad Van Grack, and Delores King Williams, and our former helpers Bo and Elaine Ayars, Judy Britt, Andrew Campbell, Cate Fox, Jim Geraghty, Duncan Hollomon, David and Leah Jeffers, Nancye Postman, Robyn Scott, Mike Tilford, and Bernice Weissburg. We should also give a tip of the Stepper hat to all the meeting planners, speakers bureaus, and airline, hotel, and out-of-town tech crew employees whose daily work has helped us take our shows on the road.

We acknowledge the heavy lifting of our own current tech crew, the fabled "roadies" of CapSteps lore, John Goings, Greg Hammon, Bob O'Hara, Jon Simler, Paul Tompros, Peter Trifiatis, Bill Turney, and those who have helped us over the years, including Ted Crews, Kim Cutlip, Drew Dedrick, John Fayer, Shannon Follin, Tammy Getz, Jim Glockner, Tom Glockner, Charles Goings, Andrew Gulino, Bo LaBorde, "Scooter" LaBorde, Van LaBorde, Brian Lady, John Lawrence, Ron Larson, Anthony Linton, Jim McCormick, Augustine Meaher, Khairullah Monawer, Jim Morris, Michael Norris, Alex Owre, David Reddish, Garth Rezek, Michael Riggs, John Roberts, Hunter Smith, Margie Tompros, Issam Tounzi, Ben Tweraser, and Sheldon White.

Our twenty-two record albums (and this CD) have required countless hours from sound technicians Remy David, Greg Hammon, Chris Murphy, and especially Jim Smith, and were produced by Reelpeople Studios, Omega Studios, and (mostly) Jim Smith's Muddy Hole Studios. All our albums have been manufactured by Richard Lion at Lion Recording Services, with very funny cover cartoons by Jim Carson, Mike Peters, and R.J. Matson—who has drawn eighteen of the twenty-two—with cover art and inset designs by Lourdes Saenz. We are grateful to our website and database gurus, Ben Armfield, Lee Hollaar, and Paul Mende.

Like the song says, there's no business like show business, but business it most definitely is. For this, we thank Jeff Hayden, Bill Lane, Alan Mertz, Harry Teter, good friends and sage advisors whose sound professional advice has been instrumental to our perseverance over the years; Harry Figgie, Jackson Frost, Sharon Rockefeller Percy, and Sarah Spitz, for making our PBS-TV and NPR-radio specials happen; our Off-Broadway producers Eric Krebs, Jonathan Reinis, Anne Squadron, and all our friends at the Houseman Theater: Marina Bridges, Jill DuBoff, Phillip George, Ken Lundie, Dave Mead, Jeffrey Richards, Jonathan Shulman, and Mark Waldrop.

Apart from business, the Capitol Steps have been pleased to sponsor the nationwide "Cappies" program for high school theater, and for this we would like to acknowledge the many thousands of donated teacher-hours and hundreds of volunteers who make this program work, especially Pati Jo Baber, Maida Belove, Mikelle Cortez, Susan Grubbs, Troy Herbort, Ed Monk, Jayvee Nable, Gael Reilly, Roger Tomhave, and Rebecca Wilburn, plus Phil Moss, Michael Peitz, and Jeffrey Leptak-Moreau of the Educational Theatre Association; Paul Gleason of the American Center for Musical Theater; with special thanks to Cappies cofounder Judy Bowns, Fairfax County School Superintendent Daniel Domenech, and Marylou Tousignant of the *Washington Post*, without whom there would be no Cappies.

We thank our cofounder Jim Aidala, for his friendship, sound advice, and colorful adjectives; former U.S. Senator Charles Percy, a classic example of how a truly nice and deeply honorable person can rise to the top in business and politics; our respective spouses, John Romano and Janie Strauss, for their loving support through thin and thick; and Bill's children Melanie, Vicky, Eric, and Rebecca, who have over the years come to grips with the fact that their father does this for a living. We thank each other, for a long partnership that, while not always easy, has been so incredibly worth it.

Lastly and especially, we thank our fans—from U.S. presidents to the people who celebrate birthdays at our shows, from corporate CEOs to the kids who sing along with our parodies and recite our "lirty dies" in the back seats of minivans. We could not have done this show, through twenty years and sixteen scandals, without you.

About the Authors

Cofounders William Strauss and Elaina Newport have been the Capitol Steps's principal writers, as well as director and producer. Together they wrote a small original paperback on the 1992 presidential campaign, *Fools on the Hill* (Longmeadow Press, 1992).

Separately, William Strauss has coauthored six books on American generational history and contemporary culture. He lives in McLean, Virginia.

Elaina Newport lives in Arlington, Virginia.

About the Capitol Steps

The Capitol Steps are former Congressional staff members who started out making up parody songs to sing at Senator Charles Percy's (R-Illinois) office Christmas party. (They were thinking of putting on a traditional nativity play, but in the entire Congress, they couldn't find three wise men or a virgin.) Twenty years later, they perform all over the country, have performed live for four presidents, and have published twenty-two CDs of their songs.

Albums by the Capitol Steps

When Bush Comes to Shove (2002)
One Bush, Two Bush, Old Bush, New Bush (2001)
It's Not Over 'Til the First Lady Sings (2000)
First Lady and the Tramp (1999)
Unzippin' My Doo-Dah (1998)
Sixteen Scandals (1997)
Return to Center (1996)
A Whole Newt World (1995)
Lord of the Fries (1994)
The Joy of Sax (1993)
All I Want for Christmas Is a Tax Increase (1993)
Fools on the Hill (1992)
76 Bad Loans (1991)
Sheik, Rattle, & Roll (1990)
Georgie on My Mind (1990)
Danny's First Noel (1989)
Stand by Your Dan (1989)
Shamlet (1988)
Workin' 9 to 10 (1987)
Thank God I'm a Contra Boy (1986)
We Arm the World (1985)
The Capitol Steps—Live (1984)

To find where songs excerpted in this book and CD are on Capitol Steps albums, please go to the Capitol Steps website: www.capsteps.com.